ENGAGING FAMILIES IN

Engaging Families in Schools is a practical resource that provides strategies and ideas that will contribute to the effective engagement of families and the involvement of parents in their child's education. Parental engagement with school staff has a significant and very positive impact on children's learning, and strategies presented have been extensively trialled in a variety of settings. Nicola S. Morgan shows school staff how to understand the importance of family engagement and evidence the outcomes. This book has been split into ten easily accessible units:

- Understanding the importance of parental engagement
- Using whole-school strategies to engage parents
- The role of the family engagement officer
- Engaging all parents
- Engaging dads

- Engaging multicultural parents
- Difficult-to-engage parents
- Working with parents to improve student attainment
- Working with parents to improve student behaviour and attendance
- Working with parents of children with additional needs.

This is a must-read guide for teaching and non-teaching staff who wish to bridge the gap between their students' school and family life and understand the effects of positive family engagement.

Nicola S. Morgan is a consultant on family engagement and behaviour management in the UK and internationally, a teacher and author. She has previously published *Better Behaviour Through Home-School Relations* (2013) and *Tackling Behaviour in your Primary School* (2012) both published by Routledge.

ENGAGING FAMILIES IN SCHOOLS

Practical strategies to improve parental involvement

Nicola S. Morgan

Routledge
Taylor & Francis Group

LONDON AND NEW YORK

First published 2017
by Routledge
2 Park Square, Milton Park, Abingdon, Oxon OX14 4RN

and by Routledge
711 Third Avenue, New York, NY 10017

Routledge is an imprint of the Taylor & Francis Group, an informa business

British Library Cataloguing in Publication Data
A catalogue record for this book is available from the British Library

Library of Congress Cataloging in Publication Data
Names: Morgan, Nicola S., author.
Title: Engaging families in schools : practical strategies to improve parental
involvement / Nicola S. Morgan.
Description: Abingdon, Oxon ; New York : Routledge is an imprint of the Taylor &
Francis Group, an Informa Business, [2017]
Identifiers: LCCN 2016025057| ISBN 9781138646247 (hardback) |
ISBN 9781138646261 (pbk.) | ISBN 9781315627632 (ebook)
Subjects: LCSH: Education–Parent participation.
Classification: LCC LB1048.5 .M65 2017 | DDC 371.19/2–dc23LC record available
at https://lccn.loc.gov/2016025057

ISBN: 978-1-138-64624-7 (hbk)
ISBN: 978-1-138-64626-1 (pbk)
ISBN: 978-1-315-62763-2 (ebk)

Typeset in Interstate
by Cenveo Publisher Services

My beautiful niece Isabelle Rose Eileen Morgan,
you carry a very special light inside you – let it shine.

CONTENTS

FOREWORD

Everyone knows that parents have an impact, for good or ill, on their children's development and educational progress. This is current common sense. Sadly, common sense has yet to catch up with the evidence on this matter and on its social significance. In a nutshell, educational achievement is the strongest predictor of social differences in, among other things, longevity, health, well-being and prosperity, and parenting practices are a major factor in shaping achievement differences.

In the UK rampant social inequality is very evident and it is a grave danger to social cohesion. Since school achievement is strongly implicated in social inequality, it falls to school leaders to take urgent and effective action to redress some of the imbalances. The evidence is clear that supporting parents is one of their best levers in this work.

In my experience, many school leaders do not fully appreciate this, and where they do, they do not have the most effective means for taking appropriate action.

Running classrooms and schools are extremely challenging tasks. Our profession has to have a very strong grasp of values, principles and relevant research. One of the most valuable things we have to offer our students is the preparedness of our professional minds. That said, our intellectual life is worthless to our students if it cannot be converted into practical action. It has been well said that a central pedagogic question is 'What do I do Monday?'

In this volume, Nicola S. Morgan answers that question comprehensively in regard to family engagement. The toolkit offered is principled, wide-ranging and evidenced-based. In addition, the book is empowering in that it provides a strong basis for further professional development in the field. There is a close and careful attention not only to 'what to do Monday' (and subsequently) but also to the crucial business of monitoring, evaluation and review. The focus throughout is on outcomes for children in terms of their attendance, behaviour and progress.

Professor Charles Desforges OBE
Emeritus Professor, University of Exeter

PREFACE AND ACKNOWLEDGEMENTS

This book has been specifically designed to provide quick and easy access to information, strategies and tips to engage parents from all walks of life.

The inspiration for writing this book came when, as a qualified teacher working with students with challenging behaviour, I realised that in order to make a sustainable difference with behaviour, attendance and standards, engaging and working with parents was key. My name is Nicola S. Morgan and I'm a teacher, international education consultant and author with over 20 years' experience working in a variety of early years, primary and secondary settings, including mainstream and special needs schools. During this time I have developed a reputation for successfully managing the most challenging classes and students, improving family engagement and motivating staff to help implement change to ensure sustainability. Throughout my career I have written a number of books and magazine articles, consulted with staff nationally and internationally, and advised on many aspects of family engagement.

This book contains not only all the all tried and tested practical and do-able approaches I have collated throughout my 20-year career, but also significant contributions from inspirational schools as well as my published works including:

- *Quick, Easy and Effective Behaviour Management Ideas for the Classroom* (Morgan 2009);
- *The 5-Step Behaviour Programme: A Whole-School Approach to Behaviour Management* (Morgan and Ellis 2009);
- *A Kit Bag for Promoting Positive Behaviour in the Classroom* (Morgan and Ellis 2011);
- *Good Choice Teddy Approach* (Morgan and Ellis 2012);
- *The Family Values Scheme* (Ellis and Morgan 2009),
- *Tackling Behaviour in Your Primary School: A Practical Handbook for Teachers* (Reid and Morgan 2012);
- *Better Behaviour Through Home–School Relations* (Ellis, Morgan and Reid 2013);
- *Family Engagement Officer's Toolkit* (Morgan 2014).

The book is written in a straightforward way to provide the reader with easy access to one-off ideas or solutions to create effective whole-school approaches to engaging families. The units have been organised as follows:

Unit 1:   Understanding the importance of parental engagement
Unit 2:   Using whole-school strategies to engage parents

To get the best out of this book, it is advisable to read all the units in turn as there are many practical ideas and strategies within each unit which can be adapted to help engage all types of parents. To accompany the book, I have put together a number of resources to help support the ideas and strategies in each unit. These can be found in the resource section of this book, on Pinterest (https://uk.pinterest.com/nsmtraining) and on the NSM Training & Consultancy website (www.nsmtc.co.uk/resources). All online resources are updated on a regular basis in order to share new ideas and good practice.

Throughout the book reference is made to 'parent(s)' as the collective term for the main caregiver of the child/young person and 'engagement' as the collective term for parental involvement and/or engagement.

I would also like to thank a number of people, schools and organisations for their contributions, strategies and case studies in writing this book. These include:

Adele Beresford-Smith (HLTA), Family Liaison Coordinator/Safeguarding Coordinator, Mill
    Green School
Alison Connor, Bensham Manor School
Beecroft Academy
Charlton Park Academy
Emma Williams, Baden Powell Primary School
Fairlands Primary School and Nursery
Hazel Earl, St Giles School
Herbert Thompson Primary
Invisible Walls Wales
Judith Stevens MBE
Kim Halford, Lyndhurst Infant School
Mel Elsey, Amy Johnson Primary School
Parc Prison, Bridgend
Penygraig Junior School
Professor Charles Desforges
Professor Ken Reid OBE
Spice Time Credits
The Education Endowment Foundation
The Welsh Assembly Government, Family and Community Engagement Toolkit for Schools
Ysgol Gynradd Gymraeg Tirdeunaw

I am particularly grateful for all the good practice shared by school staff who have attended the training courses I have led over the years. Their dedication to the schools and parents they work with has been truly inspirational and one of the driving factors of this book.

Nicola S. Morgan

LIST OF ABBREVIATIONS

AIDA	Attention, Interest, Desire and Action
ALNCO	additional learning needs coordinator
BILD	British Institute of Learning Disabilities
BME	black and minority ethnic
CAMHS	Child and Adolescent Mental Health Services
CIN	Child in Need
CQC	Care Quality Commission
CYP	children and young people
DBS	Disclosure and Barring Service
DEAR	'drop everything and read'
DfES	Department for Education and Science
DTCLA	Designated Teacher for Looked After Children
EdSRS	Education Survey & Research Service
EHC	education, health and care
FaCE	Family and Community Engagement Toolkit
FAST	Families and Schools Together
FEO	family engagement officer
FESO	family engagement support officer
IASS	Information, Advice and Support Services Network
ICT	information and communications technology
IEP	individual education plan
IIF	Investors in Families
IWW	Invisible Walls Wales
LPPA	Leading Parent Partnership Award
NCADI	National Clearinghouse for Alcohol and Drug Information (US)
NCB	National Children's Bureau
NLP	neuro-linguistic programming
NPPN	National Parent Partnership Network
Ofsted	Office for Standards in Education, Children's Services and Skills
PCP	person-centred planning
PECS	picture exchange communication system
PIP	parent involvement policy

PSP	Pastoral Support Programme
PTA	parent teacher association
RE	Religious Education
SAMEE	Scottish Association of Minority Ethnic Educators
SAMHSA	Substance Abuse and Mental Health Services Administration (US)
SATs	Standard Assessment Tests
SEAL	Social and Emotional Aspects of Learning
SEN	special educational needs
SENCO	special needs coordinator
SEND	special educational needs and disabilities
SMART	specific, measurable, achievable, relevant and time-based
SMT	senior management team
SSAT	Specialist Schools and Academies Trust
STAR	'stop, think and reflect'
TA	teaching assistant
TAC	Team Around the Child
TAF	Team Around the Family

Unit 1 Understanding the importance of parental engagement

Parental involvement and engagement

Teachers and students are the two key components of learning and school-based relationships, but there is a third party in the equation: parents. The involvement and engagement of parents in school is important for learning outcomes, attendance and behaviour, as highlighted in government policies such as Every Child Matters which followed the Children Act 2004 in the UK and the No Child Left Behind Act of 2001 in the US. There are distinct differences between parental involvement and engagement. According to Harris and Goodall (2007), parental involvement can be seen as a reactive approach, whereas engagement is a more proactive approach; other researchers state that parent involvement starts with the school and parent engagement begins with the parent.

Parental engagement involves schools working with parents to develop a professional partnership. By encouraging parents to lead in their vision and goals, so that parents start to do things for themselves rather than because school has directed them to do so, this process becomes far more sustainable.

Parental involvement involves the school leading with their own agenda, directing parents towards taking part in school meetings, events and activities, which are all selected by the school staff. If this process is not monitored and planned, parents may disengage as schools ask them to do things without first establishing a good relationship and trust. Parents may also start to over-rely on school staff to do things for them and/or to tell parents what to do and what they should be doing with their child. Joyce Epstein of Johns Hopkins University established six different types of parent involvement:

1   *Parenting.* Supporting and offering parenting skills and training courses for parents. Also providing information about how to best support their child's learning at home.
2   *Communication.* Implementing effective school-to-home and home-to-school communication systems to ensure that both parties are informed about the child's progress.
3   *Volunteering.* Providing volunteer opportunities both in school and within the community to help support the school and students.
4   *Learning at home.* Providing information and support about how parents can support their child's learning at home through homework and/or other curriculum-related activities and decisions.

5   *Decision-making.* Involving parents in decision-making opportunities throughout school – for example, being part of the governing body, PTA (parent teacher association), behaviour management review committee.

Home school partnership is not only informed by the assumption of its underlying benefits, it is also driven by the acknowledgement of the rights of parents and their needs as consumers. . . [P]arents must have a say in the way their children are taught and treated. Parents have the right to know what is going on in school and should be informed about the nature of the education their children are receiving. The general principle is that everyone who is a parent has the right to participate in decisions that affect their children's education.

(Bojuwoye 2009: 463)

6   *Collaborating with the community.* Working with the community to provide resources and services to benefit families, students and school. Also coordinating and providing support within the community to help strengthen causes and programmes.

School leaders have a critical role to play in building trust and mutual understanding between schools and communities. Trust is nurtured through relationships, through information and through knowledge.

(Riley 2009: 58–9)

The benefits of engaging families

Research has shown that family engagement is one of the strongest predictors of a student's success. When families are engaged in their child's education, attainment improves. Research conducted by Desforges and Abouchaar (2003) found that:

- Parental engagement is strongly positively influenced by the child's level of attainment: the higher the level of attainment, the more parents get involved.
- Parental engagement in the form of 'at-home good parenting' has a significant positive effect on children's achievement and adjustment even after all other factors shaping attainment have been taken out of the equation. In the primary age range, the impact caused by different levels of parental involvement is much greater than differences associated with variations in the quality of schools. The scale of the impact is evident across all social classes and all ethnic groups.

Below are more examples of the benefits gained when family engagement is present in schools.

Benefits for the school:

- Concerns can be communicated more easily and effectively.
- Parents bring skills that can benefit the school and child's learning.
- Student's attendance, behaviour and attainment improve.
- Parents can become involved with school decision-making processes.
- Parent-teacher relationships are improved.

- Parents offer more classroom support and presence on school trips.
- Parents provide more support with their child's homework.

Benefits for the students:

- Students find it easier when they receive encouragement at home.
- Attendance, behaviour and attainment improve.
- Child-parent relationships are more positive.
- Emotional literacy skills improve.
- There are more opportunities to take part in activities inside and outside school.
- Students have a more positive attitude towards school.
- There is an increased sense of security and belonging.
- Students are more likely to continue learning past the age of 16.

Benefits for the parents:

- Parents are more able to support their child's learning and development.
- They have more access to information about their child's education.
- Parents form support and networking groups with other parents.
- They build more confidence and skills.
- Parent-child relationships improve.
- More positive attitudes towards school are promoted.
- There is better parental understanding of the school process.
- Improved confidence and skills allow parents to help their child at home.

In order to capitalise on these benefits, schools need to focus on parental engagement both within and beyond the school gates and to recognise that schools and parents must form partnerships and a shared vision to achieve the desired outcomes.

> Parents are an important component within the school system, to which headteachers and teachers must be responsive. Policy-makers expect parents to be active partners who have influence over school decision-making and participate in school activities and governance.
> (Addi-Raccah and Ainhoren 2009: 805)

Barriers to parental engagement

There are many potential barriers for parental engagement, including:

- time constraints, especially for working families and single parents;
- lack of information from school or not knowing how to get involved;
- poor health and well-being;
- children attending different schools;
- family circumstances;
- caring for another member of the family;
- isolated home location and limited transport links;

- language and/or literacy barriers;
- social and cultural background;
- negative past experiences of school;
- lack of self-esteem and self-worth;
- parental uncertainty – for example, believing they are not welcome in the school;
- feeling judged by the school;
- suspicion and mistrust.

Strategic planning

Strategic planning is needed for effective involvement/engagement of parents in order to get from 'where we are now' to 'where we want to get to'. One effective system, created by Price Waterhouse in the 1980s, is the 4-Step approach, consisting of four questions:

- Where are we now?
- Where do we want to get to?
- How are we going to get there?
- How will we know when we have got there?

Step 1: Where are we now?

This stage establishes the school's present position regarding parental involvement/engagement.

Step 2: Where do we want to get to?

This stage is the school's vision of where they'd like their level of parent involvement/engagement to be.

Step 3: How are we going to get there?

This stage involves the school thinking about what process or strategy is needed to successfully reach the goal.

Step 4: How will we know when we have got there?

The last stage is achieved by analysing the data and evidence in order to measure whether Step 2 has been achieved.

Evaluating parental engagement and gathering evidence

Engaging families in school is one thing, but measuring the impact is vitally important not only for school inspections but also to secure funding from local authorities and other initiatives. In order for schools to determine the effectiveness of their parental involvement/engagement, gathering and analysing evidence is key. An ongoing plan to evaluate allows schools not only to assess effectiveness but also to identify whether areas need to be targeted differently or approaches changed. This then provides information about whether the parental involvement/engagement strategy is making a difference. Professor Charles Desforges identified a toolkit needed for schools to improve parent engagement. This includes:

- identifying parent needs;
- auditing current work;
- identifying useful initiatives;
- developing an action plan;
- undertaking evaluation;
- engaging with other organisations.

What do you want to focus on?

When looking to improve areas of parental involvement/engagement, key questions can be asked to gain an indication on the area(s) a school needs to be focusing on to generate improvement.

Does your school:

- Provide a warm welcome to all parents?
- Communicate with parents in their home languages?
- Involve parents in decision-making about how to run the school?
- Work with community groups on school and community events?
- Keep parents well informed about their child's behaviour?
- Keep parents well informed about their child's progress in school?
- Keep parents well informed about school events?
- Involve parents in everyday school activities?
- Treat all families with respect?
- Chase up parents who have not attended events to establish reasons?
- Encourage all staff take personal responsibility to engage families?
- See parents as a potential source of valuable expertise?
- Offer programmes for parents on educational and parenting issues at times and places convenient for parents?

A plan for what impact the school wants to achieve needs to be clearly defined and involve all parties, including staff, parents and governors. A parent needs assessment can also be undertaken (see p. 19). The plan can include:

- improving behaviour and well-being;
- improving attendance and lateness;
- overcoming barriers to learning so that parents can support their children's learning;
- improving students' education attainment;
- improving parental perception of the school;
- enabling parents to increase their involvement in their child's education;

- organising and running classes or events for parents;
- improving attendance at key meetings such as parents' evenings;
- organising better access to education welfare services for parents;
- planning and conducting home visits.

The stages of DIY evaluation

The Education Endowment Foundation created the DIY Evaluation Guide which provides guidance on how to conduct small-scale evaluations in schools. Table 1.1 outlines eight steps in the following three key sections: Preparation, Implementation, and Analysis and Reporting.

Gathering quantitative and qualitative information

When gathering evidence and data, ensure that both quantitative information and qualitative information are recorded.

Quantitative data come in numerical form and can be used to construct graphs etc. This form of data can be collected in many different ways such as a rating scale, closed questions

Table 1.1 Key sections of DIY Evaluation Guide

Step	Description
Stage 1: Preparation	
1. Frame your evaluation question	This is the question that your evaluation will set out to answer.
2. Decide your measure	This is what you will use to assess whether an approach has been successful, for example standardised reading, writing, mathematics or science tests.
3. Decide your comparison group	This is to understand what would have happened to learners if you had not implemented the new approach. For example, you could compare with learners in the same or a different class.
Stage 2: Implementation	
4. Conduct a pre-test	This is to understand learners' starting point on the outcome measure or to form the groups in matched designs. Learners in your intervention and comparison groups should be starting from the same point.
5. Deliver the intervention	Deliver the intervention as planned and record exactly what happened. You should ensure that your comparison group does not receive the intervention.
6. Conduct a post-test	This is to understand the impact of the intervention on the outcome measure. The post-test should be implemented at the same time with both the intervention and comparison groups.
Stage 3: Analysis and reporting	
7. Analysis and interpretation	Record the results in a spreadsheet and then calculate the effect on attainment.
8. Report the results	It is important to report the results clearly – for example, using a PowerPoint presentation.

and attendance figures. An example of quantitative data gathered at a parents' evening may include the following:

- 400 parents attended;
- 320 female adult;
- 80 male adult;
- 389 questionnaires completed.

Qualitative data comes in the form of perceptions rather than numerical forms – case studies, open-ended questions, unstructured interviews, observations – and therefore the data are harder to analyse than quantitative data. An example of qualitative data gathering at a parents' evening may include the following:

- friendly atmosphere;
- positive interactions with teachers;
- productive conversations with parents about supporting their child with home learning;
- parents keen to engage with other school activities.

Below is an example of data gathering and strategic planning from Lyndhurst Infant School.

Getting It Right: An evaluation study into the settling-in practices implemented in Reception classes at Lyndhurst Infant School

Abstract

The transition into school life can be fraught with separation anxiety and fear of the unknown for both parent and child. At Lyndhurst Infant School, the senior management team (SMT) are concerned with 'getting it right'. Investing in the family is high on the school agenda, showing commitment to the school/parent partnership by providing a family engagement officer (FEO) to assist with parental engagement within the school. The FEO devised a questionnaire in order to assess the parent's opinions of the settling-in period and the welcome meetings. All four Reception classes would take part with all parents targeted with the questionnaire. The questionnaire would also be assessing the approachability of the Lyndhurst team. The purpose of the study was to evaluate if the provision was the correct one, assess levels of service and make necessary improvement where needed. The results and feedback of this study suggest that although the parents did have concerns around their children starting school, the welcome meetings did alleviate some of these. The fact that the Lyndhurst team made themselves so readily available to them was invaluable. The purpose of the questionnaire was to make any changes necessary. Changes to everyday practices were made throughout the process.

Method/design

Participants

The study took place six weeks into the beginning of term in October 2015. In order to assess how the settling-in process for Reception classes was going in Lyndhurst Infant

School, the SMT needed to have the views and opinions of the new parents. A ten-part questionnaire, consisting of open and closed questions and including a final section for suggestions for a better service, was formulated by the FEO. The content of the questionnaire was agreed by the assistant head teacher. The focus of the questions was on the meetings before school began, the impressions the parents have of the staff team and if parents felt they were valued at school.

The questionnaires were given out one class at a time at the entrance for that particular classroom at 8.45 a.m. They were given out by the FEO who explained the importance of the parents' view and why it was important to have as many filled in as possible. The FEO explained that she would wait for the questionnaire to be completed and would collect them at 3 p.m. the same day or at the 8.45 a.m. drop-off the next morning. The FEO also waited at the entrance the following day. Those children who attended breakfast clubs were followed up by breakfast club staff. It was established that the parents who had English as a second language were able to fill in the form or had assistance from staff. This in itself it was an invaluable exercise because we identified a parent who now has all correspondence read to her by a class teaching assistant. Each class was given up to three full days and then the FEO would move on to the next class.

Data collection

When each class's questionnaire was collected in, they were evaluated first of all as a class. The process was to establish themes within classes. Small issues, such as the use of the word 'homework' in class and 'target' on the questionnaire, were rectified by clarifying what was meant by the terms. There were very few negative comments; the feedback was in the form of constructive suggestions. The negative comment was immediately given to the SMT who in turn investigated the issue and rectified it to all parties' satisfaction. After all four Reception classes' questionnaires were collected and the responses to the questions recorded, the findings were converted into percentages and graph form.

Results

Out of 115 children who are currently in 4 Reception classes 83 forms were returned, a response rate of 72 per cent.

Analysis of questions answered

Question 1

Were you worried or concerned about your child starting infant school? Please explain.

Results

Out of 83 responses, 38 (46 per cent) had concerns about their child starting school. The main concern was around the age of the children. The parents felt that their children were very young to be going to school. Separation anxiety was an issue and the parents of children with siblings in the school found this a great comfort.

Question 2

Were the meetings prior to your child starting school helpful to you? If they were, please explain how.

Results

Nine people did not answer this question. Four people did not find the meetings useful because they already had a child attending the school. Out of 83 responses, 70 (84 per cent) people said they felt the meetings were useful. They said they were informative and it was good to get to know everyone.

A suggestion was made that perhaps an additional 1:1 session would be useful.

Question 3

Did you feel the staff appeared friendly and approachable?

Results

Out of 83 responses, 81 (92 per cent) returned forms felt the staff team were approachable. One suggestion, on how the team could be more friendly and approachable, was to have more meetings at the beginning of term. The two questionnaires commenting that the team were not as approachable as they would like were immediately given to the SMT and it was discussed further with all concerned about how we could rectify this issue.

Question 4

What do you think of the settling-in period for your child?

Results

Out of 83 responses, 43 (52 per cent) returned forms felt the settling-in period was just right for their child.

Seventeen out of 83 retuned forms did not like the settling-in period at all.

Twenty-three out of 83 returned forms had mixed reviews.

Comments

- It did not fit with their family's needs.
- They already had children at Lyndhurst so everything was familiar to their child.
- Nursery children were already used to group living so they didn't need a settling-in period.

The mixed reviews said that there were indeed good and bad points to the settling-in process. Some felt it was not long enough. It was suggested for working parents that there were some childcare issues because the days were not full days. There were comments that the children could have stayed for lunch earlier. One day in particular was commented upon using the word 'chaotic'. All these comments were given to the SMT in order to evaluate arrangements made for the settling-in period.

Question 5

Have you had any issues that needed to be addressed by the senior management team?

Results

Out of 83 responses, 79 (95 per cent) of the Lyndhurst parents had not felt the need to approach the SMT.

Four parents did approach the SMT and these queries were resolved 1:1, either in a face-to-face conversation or by email, to everyone's satisfaction.

Question 6

If you had an issues or concern about your child at school, who would you approach first?

- Your child's teacher
- The office staff team
- FEO
- SMT
- I wouldn't feel confident to see anyone.

Results

Out of 83 responses, 79 (95 per cent) said that they would talk to the class teacher.

Four said they would talk to the FEO.

These questionnaires were evaluated early in the term. It was predicted that the FEO would have a greater number of approaches as the term progressed and is currently working had towards making working relationships with the new parents.

Question 7

Do you know how to help your child with their learning at home?

Have you been informed of their maths targets?

Do you practise them?

Do you share a school reading book with your child?

Results

Out of 83 responses, 75 (90 per cent) said yes to all the questions.

One said no to all the questions.

Seven said no to the math targets.

After further investigation, it was determined that some parents were not familiar with the word 'target'; the word 'homework' had been used frequently in their classroom. This issue has since been resolved and everyone is using the same terminology to avoid confusion.

Question 8

If you had an issue regarding your child's day, do you think you would be listened to?

Findings

Out of 83 responses, 82 (99 per cent) said they felt that they would be listened to with additional comments including that the staff are 'friendly and professional', that they have the highest standards and are committed. Words used to describe the Lyndhurst team included 'fantastic'; a parent would 'definitely' be listened to.

One parent remarked that they would like more communication; the SMT were made aware of this.

Question 9

Do you feel well informed about things that are happening at school?

Results

All 83 parents who returned the questionnaire felt that they are generally well informed about the events happening in school and they could identify the communication methods used:

- parent mail
- school website
- leaflets
- school notice board
- outside classroom blackboards.

Additional comments

- The school could initiate verbal reminders the day before.
- There were occasional problems with emails.
- There was a request for additional letters.

Future plans

Lyndhurst will be adding a text messaging service in 2016.

Question 10

Do you have confidence in our ability to educate and care for your child?

Results

All 83 returned forms answered yes.

Comments included that the children come first at Lyndhurst. The staff were described as relaxed and approachable, understanding and friendly. They treat the children as individuals and were patient and professional.

After the questions there was a suggestion box: 'Your views are extremely important to us. Do you have any suggestions that could help us improve the service?' Comments and feedback were:

- That the side entrance to the school was too busy.
- Email should be more available.
- A big thank you to the staff team.
- Couldn't wish for a better place.
- The children are accepted as individuals.
- Nurturing and fun environment.
- More communication at the end of the day.
- Concerns over rough play.
- Larger undercover area.
- Some parents would like to enter the building when collecting children while others liked the procedure of waiting in the allocated playgrounds. All feedback was given to the staff teams.

Discussion

The title of this research is 'Getting It Right' and, according to their parents, in the areas of most importance Lyndhurst Infant School appears to be getting it right. High percentages (over 90 per cent) were positive answers to questions about trust, confidence in staff ability and being listened to. Comments about the approachability of the staff team suggest that when there are problems, they can be resolved because the parents feel able to talk to the staff. There were a few issues being brought to the SMT at this time which were dealt with efficiently and swiftly.

The children's settling-in period and the issues parents have around the times and dates appears to be down to the family's personal circumstances. Some children are more ready for school than others. Some children appear ready or not ready for school, and when the day arrives, they surprise us all. A small minority of children were given a tailor-made induction programme as it was thought by parents, nursery staff and Lyndhurst staff that this would work best for them. This is available to any child who may be deemed unable to cope with a group transition programme.

Parents have made comments about their children staying for lunch earlier in the settling-in programme. The lunchtime period involves a lot of moving around the school building. It also includes integration with other unfamiliar adults, children, lunchtime staff and unfamiliar environments. After great consideration and knowledge-based assessment, it was determined by the SMT that it would be in the children's best interests not to overwhelm them so early in the term.

In recommending how to move forward with the findings, a more extensive explanation of why we do what we do could be implemented. A full explanation of the lunchtime routine would ensure that the parents fully understood why staying for lunch earlier may not be the answer. Lyndhurst's parents had an itinerary so that they felt prepared and were able to talk about their settling-in difficulties. The issues that were identified during the process of this research have been dealt with swiftly. The reason for this research was to make any changes necessary for next year's new intake of children, to gain invaluable feedback and to work in true partnership with our parents. As more parents experience positive transition, their apprehension about sending their child to school will lessen. It is then predicted that the concerns in question 1 will diminish.

Unit 2 Using whole-school strategies to engage parents

There are a number of key areas schools need to consider when creating a whole-school strategy for engaging parents. Staff training is one, so that everyone understands the important role parents have in their children's education, well-being, behaviour and attendance. Training in excellent parent care is a recommended place to start, as it should not be assumed that school staff are confident about working with and engaging parents.

> The most positive attitude profiles towards parental involvement were found in schools where both teachers and parents were empowered [and] there is a balance of influence between parents and teachers. . . empowering teachers is not enough; parents also need to feel that they can contribute to schools and express their 'voice'. . . in this regard, the research findings are challenging and quite optimistic. (Addi-Raccah and Ainhoren 2009: 811)

When implementing a whole-school strategy, there needs to be clarity around parent involvement and parent engagement as they are two very different areas (see p. 1). Creating a parent involvement policy is also key in this process, so that all staff and parents are aware of the school's agenda to engage. Consider whether the school culture is about 'doing with' or 'doing to' parents.

> Be honest; give respect; recognise others; show enterprise; work together; achieve more.
>   (John Lewis store)

Staff training

Training helps school staff to understand the importance of parent engagement and their role in achieving this throughout the school. This type of training helps staff to develop the following skills:

- creating a welcoming environment for parents;
- handling parent complaints;
- developing and maintaining good relationships;
- handling difficult parents without offending and frustrating them;
- understanding and addressing the needs of parents;
- providing opportunities to engage;
- learning how to build a trusting relationship.

Staff training that includes a focus on excellent parent care is an essential component to drive excellent parent engagement. Staff also need to gain an understanding and appreciation that some family backgrounds and lifestyles may be different to their own.

Why is excellent parent care important?

It can help schools:

- increase parent engagement and loyalty;
- increase the amount of time parents engage;
- generate positive word-of-mouth and reputation.

What is excellent parent care?

It includes:

- treating parents respectfully;
- following-up on feedback;
- handling complaints effectively;
- understanding parents' needs and wants;
- exceeding parent expectations;
- going above and beyond to help and support parents.

  When parents and schools interact closely together they share information among themselves and this information-sharing helps families to better understand the schools and schools to understand the families.

  (Bojuwoye 2009: 463)

Effective use of ICT

The use of ICT to promote parental engagement is key. To use ICT effectively:

- Ensure that staff have appropriate skills to use ICT to engage effectively with parents.
- Assign responsibility for ICT to key member(s) of staff.
- Carry out an assessment of where your school is regarding online reporting and communication.
- Put together a focus group including governors, staff, parents and students, to create a strategy of needs.
- Discuss with the local authority any available plans, initiatives or partnerships.
- Investigate possible solutions to support the strategy – for example, by consulting ICT suppliers, advisors and consultants.

Building trusting relationships

It is essential for staff to build trusting relationships with all parents to ensure ongoing engagement. There are many ways to do this. For example, if staff make a mistake, they should admit it, discuss resolution and move on; if staff don't know the answer, they should offer to find the answer and get back to the parent. For staff to feel confident in applying honesty in order to build trusting relationships with parents, the school culture must be one that is supportive, and for parents it must be one of acceptance, communication and value towards all.

Engaging staff, engaging parents

There is a direct correlation between how staff are engaged and how they engage parents. This is mainly due to the fact that staff feel their opinions and ideas are important. Organisations that have a higher level of staff involvement in decision-making show higher levels of staff motivation and satisfaction. Below are suggestions on how to achieve this.

The Disney model

Walt Disney organised his creative workforce in a certain way to guarantee creative outcomes. He created three rooms (these could be three boards on the wall) and each room had different function.

The Dreamer Room

This stage was for pure creativity. Staff list ideas with no limitations – for example, if you had a magic wand. This helps to build a bank of creative ideas full of passion and enthusiasm. Suggested questions to ask at this stage are:

- What do we want to achieve?
- Why do we want to achieve it?
- What is the solution?
- What does the solution look like?
- What are the outcomes for achieving the solution?

The Realist Room

This stage looks at the ideas from the Dreamer Room in a more logical planning style. Timeframes and milestones for progress are determined. This stage is about 'how?' Suggested questions to ask at this stage are:

- How can this idea be implemented?
- How will we know if the idea has been implemented successfully?
- Who will champion the idea?
- What is the timeline to apply this idea?
- How will we evaluate the idea?

The Critic Room

The last stage looks critically at the proposed action plan and decides whether it can be achieved. This becomes a safe process, even though it is labelled as the Critic Room, because it is the project not the person who is being examined. Suggested questions to ask at this stage are:

- What could go wrong with the idea?
- Who will the idea affect and how will it affect them?
- Is there anything missing which could cause the idea to fail?
- Why can't we apply it?
- Are there any weaknesses in the plan?

You are the parent!

In groups, ask staff to take off their professional hats and step into the shoes of a parent. Then ask the question: 'How would you as a parent like to be engaged in your child's school?' Record all responses on flipchart paper.

When completed, ask staff on a separate piece of flipchart paper the question: 'How does your school engage parents?'

Looking at both pieces of flipchart paper, ask staff to discuss whether question 1 is addressed in question 2 and, if not, what changes the school can make to meet the needs of parents.

You are my guest

Ask staff to make a list of things they would do in preparation for a guest visiting their home. Consider using the Disney model, then implement. With this list, identify areas that can be implemented in school.

Ideas board

Provide a staff ideas board for sharing and learning new strategies that support parent engagement – this can be a physical board in the staff room or an online board – for example, on Pinterest: https://uk.pinterest.com/nsmtraining.

Family engagement champions

Although family engagement is the responsibility of the whole school staff, in order to ensure that goals are met and achieved and that the school's vision in this area is consistent and sustainable, it is important that it is led by a senior leader (head teacher) as well as a member of staff whose main role is family engagement (family engagement officer – see Unit 3).

School improvement

Include in the school improvement plan an area to involve parents so that they can feel part of and participate in the school improvement planning process. Allocate parent roles and responsibilities and invite their input.

School walk assessment

A good way to assess how parent-friendly the school is would be to assign a small team of parents, staff and students to agree and make a list of what they'd like to examine and then do a walk-through of the school. Within the team, groups can be allocated certain areas to focus on – for example, school environment, materials available for parents including policies, school staff and practices. The team can then formulate an action plan based on their findings. Below are a few examples.

School environment

- Can you see any signs to welcome you into school?
- Can you find where to park?
- Are you able to find the reception area?
- Do you know where to sign in?
- Do you know where the toilets are?
- Can you see any signs as you're leaving the school to welcome you back?
- Can you answer the questions above if:
  - English is not your first language?
  - You are blind/visually impaired?

School grounds

Parents need to feel safe and also want to know their child is safe, so well-maintained school grounds, appropriate lighting, secure games and reception areas are all important. Survey parents to gauge their thoughts and make amendments where necessary. Ask a member of staff to take responsibility to check main entrance and school grounds every morning and afternoon, and complete the following checklist:

- Main entrance clean and tidy.
- Grounds near the front entrance litter-free.
- Driveway clear and litter-free.

Written materials including policies

- Are written materials available in different languages?
- Are written materials designed for parents who are visually impaired, dyslexic, etc.?
- On request, were you given your chosen policy?

- Are school policies provided to parents in a format they can understand?
- Was there a selection of reading materials available in the waiting room/foyer?
- Do parents receive information from school on a regular basis?

School staff

- Did you receive a warm and friendly welcome from all reception staff?
- Were staff able to answer any questions and/or concerns in a courteous manner?
- Did you see a list of staff names and photos so that you were aware of who you were meeting?
- Was your phone call answered in a timely fashion?
- When you made a phone call, were you given the required information in a courteous way?
- Are staff members friendly? Do they smile?
- Did staff members ask whether you need help?

Practices

- Was the sign-in procedure efficient and straightforward?
- Were you given a school information pack?
- How user-friendly was the school information pack?
- Are the transition practices of a good standard for both parent and student?
- How are parents encouraged to participate at school on a regular basis?
- What practices does the school have in place to ensure effective communication with parents?

Action plan

Following staff input, creating an action plan is the next step in addressing the 'who', 'by when' and 'how' plans to improve parent engagement. Be realistic about what your school can accomplish and set both short-term and long-term goals. Good practice in schools has shown that by planning three months in advance for parent events, meetings and activities, these have been well received by parents because they are able to plan ahead, arrange time off work, organise babysitters, etc.

Parent needs assessments

How can the school meet parents' needs if no one knows what they are? According to O'Mara et al. (2010), interventions are more likely to be effective when they are informed by the views of parents identified by means of a thorough needs assessment conducted on a regular basis. This is also more important than ever for the school inspection process. When designing your parent needs assessments, make sure that it will give you actionable feedback. Ask more open questions than closed ones.

Parental engagement interventions are more likely to be effective if they are informed by a comprehensive needs analysis and are targeted at particular groups of parents.

(Goodall and Vorhaus 2011)

Below are some assessment suggestions.

Online surveys

Online surveys can be used to establish parents' needs as well as parental perception. Below are just a few examples of how these can be done:

- Survey Monkey
- School Survey Experts
- Keele University School Surveys
- Kirkland Rowell Surveys.

Face-to-face surveys

These surveys are particularly effective as parents are not required to fill in a survey form but instead answer questions verbally, whether face-to-face or over the phone.

Our guest signing-in sheet

Select two or three parents who have signed into school as a guest and call them to ask them about their experience. This approach can generate useful information, especially if they are contacted on the day they have visited. Relay the information to staff and celebrate the 'good stuff' and problem-solve the areas needing improvement. If applicable, send out the 'You Said – We Did' approach (see p. 50).

The 1 to 5 scale feedback cards

This is a great way to collect information. Just ask parents to rate listed questions on a card. These can be given out at reception while a parent is waiting.

1   Poor
2   Average
3   Quite good
4   Good
5   Very good

Post-it!

In the reception area, create a feedback wall with one question clearly printed, for example: 'How does our school communicate with you? How can we improve?' Provide three different-coloured packs of Post-it notes – for example, green = very well; yellow = OK; red = poorly.

Invite parents to choose a coloured Post-it and either place it on the feedback wall as it is or write on it a suggestion for improvement and hand in to reception.

Counter vote

Place three large see-through tubes all of the same size in the reception area. Label the tubes 'Very Good', 'OK' and 'Poor', and write a question above the tubes – for example, 'How helpful are the staff at our school?' Provide a container of plastic tokens and invite parents to place a token in the tube to score their rating.

Mystery shopper

Just as businesses use mystery shoppers to tell them whether their product or service is up to scratch, schools can use mystery shoppers to help establish whether the school is parent-friendly. Ask a member of staff from another school to pose as a parent and evaluate the welcome they receive, whether everything is clearly signposted and so on. They can record their findings and return these to the school.

Focus group

Organise a focus group within the school and invite parents to take part in order to establish what they think about certain aspects of school. Ask a member of staff to be the facilitator and to explore the reasons behind parents' thoughts in order to address them through the school improvement plan.

It's good to talk

Communication is essential for successful parent engagement, so get feedback from parents regarding their preferred way of being contacted by the school. Investigate technology that can assist you with communication and trial it with your parents to establish its effectiveness.

Parent involvement policy

Developing a parent involvement policy (PIP) is a great way to ensure a sustainable and effective approach to engaging all different kinds of parents. The policy should include information on how the school will address the following issues: communication, parenting, skills, children's learning, volunteering, school decision-making and community involvement. Below are a few examples.

Communication

Implement effective communication channels between the home and the school in order to provide information about the children's curriculum, progress, behaviour, attendance, interests, activities and other school-based events, including any external trips or visits.

Parenting

Provide information and training for parents about how to create a positive learning environment at home, as well as the best ways of supporting their children's school and schooling.

Children's learning

Provide information and training for families to help with their child's education on issues such as homework.

Volunteering

Create opportunities for parents or carers to volunteer through participation in supportive roles, activities and events at the school.

School decision-making

Good decision-making is about providing opportunities for parents or carers to become involved in educational advocacy and decision-making on issues that affect their children's education, such as invoking and implementing new school policies.

Community involvement

Create links with community support groups, agencies and initiatives to help strengthen family and school partnerships.

Parent involvement policy example

Below is an example of a PIP from Beecroft Academy in Bedfordshire.

Parent Involvement Policy, Beecroft Academy, Bedfordshire

Introduction

All parents and carers are equally valued as part of our school community. Children's learning is improved when we work in partnership with their parents or carers and their wider family. We therefore believe in close cooperation with all families and in regular consultation between the home and the school.

Aims and objectives

Our aims through parental involvement are:

- to enhance the learning experiences of all students;
- to encourage parents and carers to be involved in the children's learning;

- to provide a partnership between home and school, seeking to ensure that families feel welcome and valued;
- to ensure that maximum use is made of all these adults' skills to enrich learning opportunities.

The school's 'open door' policy

The staff and governors at Beecroft Lower School (now known as Beecroft Academy) offer an 'open door' policy to all parents/carers; this means that parents/carers can access the school and school staff at all reasonable and convenient times. School staff will work hard to help all parents/carers to the best of their ability; they will be happy to listen to good news and will also endeavour to deal with questions, queries and concerns in a positive and swift manner. Ultimately, all school staff will help all parents/carers in any way they can. If the member of staff is unable to help, then they will seek information and advice from other relevant parties and the parent/carer will receive a response in due course. If a parent/carer needs to speak to a member of the school staff, their first point of contact is their child's class teacher.

Parents/carers can contact their child's class teacher in a number of ways, including:

- writing a message in their child's Home Learning Diary;
- speaking to the class teacher on the playground before school when they are on duty;
- asking the 'before school duty teacher' to pass on a message to their child's class teacher, asking them to make contact;
- speaking to their child's class teacher at the end of the day after the rest of the children have left the building;
- contacting the school office by telephone and leaving a message for their child's class teacher to contact them.

Note. Parents/carers will avoid coming into the school office to alleviate congestion in the school corridor.

Nearly all questions and queries will be sorted out by a child's class teacher. The school's office staff will only be able to help with matters related to the office, such as uniform and free school meals. To avoid congestion in the corridors, it is recommended that parents/carers speak to the office staff about such matters either by phone or by sending a note to their child's class teacher.

Also, any parent/carer asking to speak to a member of the senior team, including the headteacher, will be asked if they have spoken to their child's class teacher first. If they have not spoken to their child's class teacher, they will be asked to do so before an appointment will be made with a member of the senior team.

If a parent/carer does require an appointment with the headteacher, they will need to contact the school by telephone and ask to speak to the headteacher's personal assistant. S/he will record a reason for the appointment and will organise an appropriate date and time.

Communication

School staff work hard to communicate effectively with parents/carers. They do this in a number of ways:

- school prospectus;
- letters;
- flyers;
- face-to-face discussion opportunities;
- at school events and celebrations, e.g. the governors' annual report to parents/carers;
- via the schools website at www.beecroftacademy.co.uk.

When communicating with parents/carers, either face-to-face, on the telephone or in writing, school staff will be polite and respectful. It is expected that all parents/carers will also behave in a polite and respectful manner when speaking to children, staff, governors and other parents/carers from the school. A 'zero tolerance' approach will be taken with any parent/carer considered to be behaving in a verbally or physically aggressive, abusive or violent manner. Parents/carers who behave in this way will be asked to leave the building and the police may be called. Also, the headteacher, supported by the governing body, will contact the local authority to seek legal advice with regard to action that will be taken in response to this type of behaviour.

Involvement in children's learning

In order to find out about their child's learning, parents/carers can:

- speak with their child's class teacher informally;
- attend parent/carers' evenings twice a year;
- attend sessions where they are invited to look at their child's work/books twice a year;
- read their child's annual report card;
- read their child's annual report;
- attend a wide range of events, assemblies, performances, etc. to see their child participating in school life.

Parents/carers are asked to sign a Home–School Learning Agreement when their child starts at the school. This agreement makes clear the expectations of the school in terms of how a parent/carer should support their child's learning.

In order to support their child's learning, parents/carers can:

- ensure that their child is in school every day, on time;
- carry out the daily home learning activities suggested by the school (e.g. reading);

- attend regular curriculum workshops that are organised to assist parents/carers in supporting their child's learning;
- support their child with the focused, enrichment activities that are sent home from school.

School staff value the support that is given to children at home by their parents/carers as this helps children to make progress in great strides in school.

Involvement in the life of the school

School visits

Parents/carers are more than welcome to visit the school and spend time in the classrooms in order that they can understand school life and the provision that is being made for the children. Appointments are made via the school office.

Volunteering to help in school

Parents/carers are warmly invited to help in school with activities such as educational trips, supporting children's learning in the classroom or hearing children read. Parents/carers are also invited, where appropriate, to visit classes and groups of children to give talks or demonstrations on areas of interest in which they are experts. Any parent/carer who is interested in helping in school should contact their child's class teacher.

Note. It is necessary to organise a personal background check with the Disclosure and Barring Service (DBS) on any person who will be working with children in school prior to that person's involvement.

The Friends of Beecroft

The school has a successful group of parents/carers and staff called the 'Friends of Beecroft', who work very hard to offer exciting enrichment opportunities for the children and raise money for the school. Any parent/carer wishing to join, or offer support to, the 'Friends of Beecroft' should telephone the school office and ask for further details. This body of parents/carers and school staff works voluntarily to raise money for the school.

Parent/Carer Forum

The school offers an opportunity for parents and carers to contribute to the development of the school provision by taking part in the Parent/Carer Forum. Parents/carers can explore a range of topical school issues and provide information and ideas to support improvement.

The school's extended service

The Beehive SureStart Children's Centre: Beecroft School offers a wide range of activities in which parents/carers, children and families can get involved. For further details, contact the Beehive SureStart Children's Centre staff on 01582 699092.

The governing body

The governing body will seek out parents/carers who are willing to serve as members of the school governing body when a position becomes available. Parent governors represent the views of parents/carers.

Consultation

The school will make every effort to consult parents and carers, both formally and informally, about their views on school life, children's learning and new initiatives. Periodically, the school will seek parental views more formally, through an annual survey or a questionnaire on a particular theme. The school values regular feedback, and will make every effort to act on parents/carers' views, wherever possible. Parents/carers are welcome to provide such feedback through the formal channels, as detailed above, or on an ad hoc basis. The school welcomes regular feedback both about positive aspects or where improvements could be made.

Finding out about the school

The governing body publishes 'The School Profile' once a year; this is shared at the governors' Annual Report to Parents/Carers. After an Ofsted inspection, parents/carers will receive a summary of the findings; the report can also be accessed online at www.ofsted.gov.uk.

Monitoring and review

The headteacher will monitor the implementation of this policy and will submit periodic evaluation reports on its effectiveness to the governing body.

This policy will be reviewed every two years (or earlier if necessary).

Mr J. Hughes (Headteacher)

Marketing

Les Brown, a motivational speaker from the US, said that marketing is all about telling your 'story'. Most people want to know three things before they buy into your service: Who are you? Can I trust you? Why should I bother? As a school, telling your 'story' through marketing initiatives is key, but the 'story' requires thought followed by a plan to ensure consistency throughout, taking into account the school's ethos, culture and values. Below are a few suggestions.

Family-friendly school

In order to engage families, schools need to convey a family-friendly message, which needs to be communicated alongside the school name, on letterheads, the website, email signatures, etc. For example:

- Name of school – A family-friendly school
- Name of school – Strong partnerships with families
- Name of school – Striving to be a family-friendly school
- Name of school – Staff, families and students together

Banner it!

Using banners to advertise forthcoming events for families is very powerful, but remember to include a 'call for action'. Think about what message you'd like to get across to your families within a few seconds, then put together a calendar and schedule of banner content.

For families who drive past your school, a banner can engage, inform and invite. Below are a few examples of a call to action. We invite you to...

- contact us today ...
- come in for a ...
- tell us what you think ...
- tell us how are we doing ...
- learn the top three tips on ...
- sign up while you can/before it's too late
- ask not what your school can do for you but what you can do for your school! So what can you do?

Banners can also entertain and inspire, for example:

- word of the week;
- quote of the month;
- interesting facts.

Networking between schools

Networking and collaborating with other local schools is a very powerful resource when engaging with families. Networking allows for sharing knowledge, opportunities, resources and good practice.

Include all

Ensure your school welcomes all family members – not just parents but also carers, grandparents, step-parents, kinship carers, foster carers, special guardians, respite carers and birth parents. It is important that staff understand the legal responsibilities of carers in particular, and make it clear that your school is for carers as well as parents.

Signage

Signage around the school is a very important form of communication to encourage and support families. A good place to start is to audit with the school council all the signage around your school and change any negative signs to positive. For example, instead of 'No parking' 'No entry', say 'Parking for families is to the side of the school'. Also consider the following:

- Can you see any signs to welcome you into school?
- Can you find where to park?
- Are you able to find the reception area?
- Do you know where to sign in?
- Do you know where the toilets are?
- Can you see any signs as you're leaving the school to welcome you back?

Can you answer the questions above if:

- English is not your first language?
- you are blind/visually impaired?

If you have answered no to any of the above, then put a plan in place to address this.

You are here!

Many buildings, amusement parks and shopping malls display maps with an arrow showing where you are. This helps the customer navigate successfully, and feel confident and well informed about their experience. Why not create such maps and display the in schools/colleges?

- Work with staff and parents to decide where these maps are placed.
- Ensure map shows directions to frequently visited locations such as the main office.
- Include the school name and logo on the map.
- Find sponsorship from local businesses to help with the map production.

Car park

For some parents, it may be confusing and frustrating to find out where to park when visiting the school. Can you address this need by providing designated parking areas for families – 'Family parking' – which are clearly signed?

Audit your signs

Check all signs around the school and where possible make them positive rather than negative. For example:

- instead of 'No parking' – 'Guest parking';
- instead of 'No entry' – 'Reception this way'.

Goodbye and come back

Always invite families to visit again. When a parent leaves school, encourage staff to say something like 'Thank you for visiting. Come back again soon' or 'Thank you for being our guest. When will we see you again?' This can also be achieved by displaying signs on the exit of the school saying 'Thank you for coming. See you next time.'

The welcome

First impressions count, and the way your parents are met and greeted at your school will have a big impact on how they engage. People tend to make judgements about each other and the environment within the first minute. Negative or positive first impressions can easily become lasting impressions and can make a difference between engagement and lack of engagement. It is therefore critical that we get it right first time. Remember that no detail is ever too small, so consider what parents see, hear, smell, touch and feel. Below are some top tips.

Welcoming reception area

When a parent comes into school, their first port of call is usually the reception area and it is likely their first impression is made there. Consider the following:

- a warm friendly welcome from all reception staff;
- appropriate seating and lighting;
- clear signage – where to sign in;
- engaging, calming music being played (e.g. local radio);
- selection of reading materials on a coffee table:
  - school brochures
  - magazines
  - newspapers
  - leaflets
  - TV screen showing upcoming events
  - display on family achievements
  - a book of students' success.

> It takes 20 years to build a reputation and five minutes to ruin it. If you think about that, you'll do things differently.
>
> (Warren Buffett)

Open all hours

Make sure parents are aware of the school opening and closing times. This can be achieved by including the information on every piece of documentation that goes out to parents. It is also a good idea to publish emergency and after-hours phone numbers. If it has been high-lighted on a parental needs assessment, could your school employ a member of staff to work a few hours after school so that they can address any parental concerns?

What's playing?

Some parents may feel more comfortable if your reception area has local radio playing rather than Mozart, and magazines on the coffee table rather than just the school prospectus. It will help if there are toys for toddlers to play with, information in community languages and posters inviting families to join in a wide range of activities. Also consider having the school orchestra play up-to-date music when parents arrive for meetings as this well help them feel at ease.

Guess who?

Knowing who's who within a school can be quite stressful for some parents, especially when they've never met a member of staff before. In the foyer, display photos of all staff members including name, job role and department. Replicate this information on the school website, with an additional link to the family engagement officer (see p. 34).

Contacting the school

Parents will want to contact the school in many ways – for example, face-to-face, online, mail, phone and email. All these channels of communication need to be open, easily accessible and interlinked. To ensure parent satisfaction and engagement, respond in the agreed timely fashion, even if it is to say the information they have requested will take some time to collate.

Telephone

When a parent takes the time to contact the school, in most cases they are looking for some type of assistance. It is therefore important that questions, concerns or queries are addressed in a timely manner so that the parent feels listened to and valued.

What constitutes a 'timely manner' is open to interpretation, so setting clear expectations about responding to parents is critical. Consider the timings for the following:

- responding to a voice message;
- getting back to a parent regarding information requested;
- referring the call to another member of staff and that member of staff phoning the parent.

Telephone handover

Sometimes a parent will phone the school with a specific request which needs to be passed on to another member of staff. Put a system in place so that the parent only has to explain the request once rather than repeat it to a number of different people.

Website

Keep the school website up to date and make sure it clearly displays ways to contact the school. Parents need to feel they have a real person on hand to help if needed. The values and ethos of the school as 'family friendly' should also be clearly communicated. Consider the following:

- Create and recreate and update your website and other technology used to communicate and engage with parents.
- Develop a plan to monitor updating.
- Survey parents often as to the effectiveness of the technology being used – and respond accordingly.
- Read website reports to determine the effectiveness of your website and monitor visits.

Reception staff

In order to develop an excellent parent care service within the school, valuable information can be gained from talking to parent-facing staff (reception staff) on a regular basis. Information can then be collated on what parents are feeling, using the results to improve your service.

Take a tour

Ask a group of students to create a film of the outside and inside of the school, providing a guided tour and opportunity for parents to look round the school from the comfort of their own home. The film can be put on the school website and a link sent out to all parents via text or email, with the invitation to 'Click here to take a guided tour of our school'. Include the following:

- entering through the school gates;
- locations of designated parking for parents;
- the reception area and staff;
- the headteacher's office;
- the family engagement officer's office;
- staff introductions;
- toilets;
- school hall.

The school greeter

As well as having a warm and friendly reception area, having a member of staff at the entrance of the school to greet parents and students every morning and at the end of the school day not only conveys a warm welcome/goodbye but also provides an excellent opportunity to deal with any queries parents may have. The superstore Walmart has a greeter at the entrance of every store. Staff also wear badges saying 'How can I help you?' or 'I'm here to help you'. Having that personal interaction can build trusting relationships, and when you have trust, you have engagement. Consider the following:

- Invest time teaching and providing your new greeters with information about your school.
- Use greeters fluent in different languages – advertise this to families.
- Have a member of staff at each door and in the car park.
- Families appreciate when staff value their children enough to meet and greet them each morning.
- Target school locations where families and students gather on a regular basis.
- Designate staff members to be at such locations each day to greet each student and family and provide general supervision.
- Wave and smile at every student and adult who passes.
- Headteachers also need to participate in the meet and greet.

Be our guest

- During staff training ask groups to discuss what they do in preparation for a 'guest' visiting their home.
- Instead of referring to parents entering school as 'visitors', refer to them as 'guests'. This is something Disney have been doing for many years as they want people to feel welcome and part of the experience.
- Title your signing-in book 'Be our guest and sign in'. You can also provide badges with the words 'You're Our Guest' clearly printed.
- Explain the locked gate and signing-in process and that the school cares about the safety of students and of guests, which is why it is important for them to sign in.
- Utilise the signing-in process by handing a parent up-to-date information about school contacts and event dates. This can be done in the form of a bookmark or fridge magnet – a quick and effective way to share information.

Parent engagement awards

Awards are a great way of consolidating good practice as well as publicising to parents how good the school is and how it will benefit families. There are a number of awarding bodies which assess and award schools' achievement in effectively engaging families. Here are some examples:

- Investors in Families (IIF) is a quality mark that recognises the work that schools and other settings undertake with families to improve outcomes for children and young people. The quality mark is awarded to schools and other settings that demonstrate a commitment to working with families and evidence of the activities that indicate close working with families. IIF Wales is a national scheme, with national standards, that is accredited locally.

- The Leading Parent Partnership Award (LPPA) is a national award that provides a coherent framework through which schools, early years settings and other educational organisations can deliver effective parental engagement from early years to post-16.
- The SSAT (Specialist Schools and Academies Trust) offer schools the Parental Engagement Quality Standard award which recognises and celebrates schools' family engagement work.

Parental engagement in children's learning makes a difference – it is the most powerful school improvement lever we have.

(Harris and Goodall 2007: 70)

Unit 3: The role of the family engagement officer

The role

Family engagement officers (FEOs) work in partnership with families, parents and students in a school context, helping to improve behaviour and attendance and to overcome barriers to learning so that parents can increase their involvement in their child's education, both at school and at home.

> Building home–school links through out of hours clubs, parenting classes, extended schools and outreach work can lead to improvements in completion of homework, learning behaviours and improved attendance.
>
> (Goodall and Vorhaus 2011)

FEOs typically work to tackle underachievement, enabling students to access educational opportunities and overcome barriers to maximise learning and participation. FEOs work directly and non-judgementally with parents, empowering them and their families to get the most out of the educational opportunities available. FEOs work with parents and children to:

- improve behaviour and attendance;
- overcome barriers to learning so that parents can support their children's learning;
- enable parents to increase their involvement in their child's education, both at school and at home.

FEOs may work in a single school or in a cluster of schools. They may previously have worked in education, health or social care, or they may be parents. Within the school(s), the FEO will work with a range of staff; outside school, they may work with agencies supporting parents and children. The FEO may offer one-to-one support to parents to engage them in their children's learning, or work with groups of parents.

The role of FEO varies, depending on the needs of the school(s) in which they work; for this reason, a job description for the FEO is essential. The FEO's day-to-day tasks could include:

- organising and running classes or events for parents;
- encouraging attendance at parents' evenings;
- offering one-to-one assistance to parents;
- contacting parents of absent students;

- arranging access to education welfare services or other relevant specialist services for parents;
- planning and conducting home visits.

FEOs are likely to work with a wide range of partners and practitioners from the statutory, voluntary and private sectors. The services provided may include parenting programmes, health-related services or enrichment activities. It will be part of the FEO's role to establish links on behalf of the school with all such partners and consider how these partnerships can support parents.

It is important that the work done with families is recorded effectively and securely, enabling easy access to the information and minimising the risk of essential information being lost or overlooked. The best way to do this is to keep all the information in a family file. Filing systems should be organised so that the information can be easily retrieved and understood. Having a clear and standard procedure for creating and maintaining files is recommended. For example:

- Maintain a separate file or section in a file for each student and family member. To help with targeting families, set up a system through which you can identify your target families and track how you get on – for example, add parents who are engaging in a 'green folder', parents who are starting to engage in an 'orange folder' and parents who are not engaging in a 'red folder'. These traffic-light folders provide an easy system to move parents according the engagement and provide a clear focus for the FEO.
- Keep third-party and student protection information in a removable section to comply with legislation regarding access to records.
- Where possible, keep any paper records in relation to an individual student in one file.
- Ensure that recording is factual and accurate. The recorder (FEO) should print and sign their name with the correct date and time the recording took place.
- Adhere to all data protection legislation. The FEO should produce a progress report on each case at a time agreed with the headteacher. At this time the headteacher should sign off and pass any necessary information to the relevant agencies.

Recording systems should be clear and simple. The purpose of recording is to:

- record any involvement the FEO has had with the family;
- record outcomes for the student;
- feed information back to the school;
- record major incidents and decisions, which may include confidential information;
- record contact between the FEO and other agencies;
- help the headteacher and FEO to monitor progress with the family;
- allow the family to see what progress has been made;
- provide evidence for care proceedings and safeguarding meetings.

Records should:

- begin with the first contact and end with the last;
- be completed in collaboration with families and other agencies;
- provide basic essential information on the family and the involvement of other agencies.

All entries must:

- be clearly written in ink if handwritten or be printed off if electronic;
- be signed and dated by the recording member of staff (all alterations must also be signed, dated and timed);
- be factual and not include opinions unless they are relevant and are clearly attributed;
- be clear, concise and comprehensive;
- make it clear which individual is being referred to (e.g. by using names or titles rather than pronouns such as 'he' or 'she');
- avoid using abbreviations, jargon or irrelevant speculation.

All files should include:

- a label on the front including the name of the family, dates of birth of the children, address, ID number, the date the case was opened and closed, and the name of the FEO;
- a first page consisting of a chronology of significant events, briefly listing the date and type of contact;
- a referral form;
- basic family information – family members, ages, etc.;
- an action plan, including review;
- a consent to information form, signed by the parent (this should be reviewed with parents on an annual basis);
- sections for each family member;
- working agreement;
- family plan, reviews, case summaries and transfers;
- recording sheets, dated and signed (in order to comply with data protection regulations, there should be a separate section for each student);
- reports from other agencies and minutes of meetings with other agencies;
- a separate third-party confidential section for the recording of any sensitive information.

Engaging and communicating with parents

The foundation of the FEO's work is effective engagement. Family engagement must be underpinned by:

- the school's values and principles, which guide the work of the FEO;
- respect for parents' rights;
- support for parents in meeting their responsibilities;
- equal opportunities.

Although FEOs may not have the expertise and knowledge to offer assistance in every aspect of a parent's life, they should know how to access the necessary support, and know how and when to involve others. The following approach will help in this:

- Assessing the needs of the parent: working with the parent, and where appropriate the wider community, to identify needs within the community context.

- Planning in partnership with the parent to meet their needs: determining which other services need to be involved and what each provides.
- Liaising with the relevant services and contacting the most appropriate individual for the particular support required.
- Asking for the support required: knowing exactly what is being asked for and whether it is within the remit of the service.
- Advocating not on behalf of any one person, but working to ensure that the parent's views are heard, understood and responded to.
- Negotiating with the relevant service to provide that support. (This negotiation might involve offering support, resources or future joint working to obtain what is required.)

Understanding boundaries

Professional boundaries are the guidelines, expectations and rules that set the ethical and technical standard in the school environment. They set limits for safe, acceptable and effective behaviour by FEOs. Professional boundaries mean:

- clearly established limits that allow for safe connections between the FEO, parents and students;
- being with the parent/student, not becoming the parent/student;
- being friendly, not friends;
- knowing where the role of the FEO begins and ends;
- clearly understanding the limits and responsibilities of the FEO role as a service provider.

Boundaries are important in:

- modelling to the parent/student healthy communication and professional relationships;
- avoiding the 'rescuer' role;
- allowing the FEO to remain focused on their responsibilities to the parent/student and the provision of helpful and appropriate services;
- avoiding compassion fatigue;
- maintaining appropriate and transparent communication;
- supporting teamwork within the school;
- maintaining physical and emotional safety.

The role of the FEO should be established as early as possible in the professional relationship (i.e. at the initial meeting) with the parent (e.g. by clear agreements about the FEO's availability for meetings). When boundary issues or warning signs appear, these should be addressed immediately. A sensitive approach should be taken, with emphasis on the importance of maintaining healthy boundaries. These are often sensitive relationships, and it may be necessary to frequently clarify the role and boundaries and ask the parent to confirm understanding. If the situation becomes uncomfortable, the FEO should discuss this with the headteacher. An effective tool to use during meetings with parents is a 'Working Agreement' which is a contract between parent and FEO to establish expectations and boundaries. Two copies are printed; one is given to the parent and the FEO files the other. The contract can include the following:

1. Full name of parent
2. Full name of child and date of birth
3. Home address
4. Telephone number, mobile phone number, email address
5. Responsibilities of the FEO:
   - to provide you with professional and respectful care
   - to accept and listen to you in a non-judgemental way
   - to keep confidentiality, providing it is in line with school policies; if information is given which indicates that the law has been broken and/or is a safeguarding concern, then the FEO will report to the appropriate body
6. Responsibilities of the parent:
   - to be open and willing to share your concerns
   - to ask questions when you don't understand or when you need clarification
   - to keep appointments or to give at least 24 hours advance notice if you need to cancel or reschedule a meeting
7. FEO's signature and date
8. Parents' signature and date

Considerations when engaging parents

FEOs can help to engage parents by encouraging them to:

- take an interest in the day-to-day life of the school;
- read with their child;
- find opportunities to use maths in everyday tasks at home;
- attend parents' evening and talk to teachers;
- visit museums and galleries;
- create a quiet time and place for homework;
- support and encourage the completion of homework and course work;
- help with revision;
- understand their child's behaviour;
- get their child to school on time;
- help their child to set goals and raise their child's aspirations.

The FEO will also be involved in:

- organising induction programmes for starting school or starting a new school;
- formulating and implementing new policies in schools;
- planning parent–teacher events, end-of-term events;
- parents' evening and open days;
- transition points such as a change of key stage.

How the FEO will engage and communicate with parents will differ from family to family, taking into account such factors as:

- literacy levels;
- language;
- education level and confidence;
- personal beliefs;
- personality;
- work and time pressures;
- childcare needs;
- causes of family stress such as divorce, bereavement, substance misuse, physical and mental health issues;
- previous experiences with the family.

The FEO can help to make engagement easier for parents by:

- ensuring that they feel comfortable and at ease;
- communicating with them in the most appropriate way;
- checking that they understand the process of the engagement;
- checking that they understand the role of the FEO;
- discussing issues of, and limits to, confidentiality;
- establishing acceptable working rules;
- making access easier, particularly taking into consideration childcare needs, transport, time and location.

While engaging parents, the FEO should try to gather the following information from them and other practitioners:

- understanding of the perspectives and views of the parents;
- awareness of the family set-up (e.g. who has parental responsibility);
- an appreciation of the value system of the parents;
- awareness of the beliefs and customs of relevant ethnic groups;
- awareness of specific gendered experiences and needs of mothers and fathers;
- strategies for working with specific groups of parents (e.g. young parents, non-resident parents, fathers);
- the support and information available to parents;
- awareness of any relevant information sharing and safeguarding policy.

Types of support

Self-support

Some parents may only be seeking information or wanting to know how to access specific support. Many parents will be independent after they have been signposted to the right support.

The involvement of the FEO in such cases may be to provide leaflets or lists of relevant services. If parents do not have access to the Internet, they may only require the support of the FEO to provide information about where they can get free Internet access (e.g. through the school or local library).

Peer support

FEOs may facilitate peer groups if a sufficient number of parents would be interested in this kind of support.

Direct support

For some parents, a level of involvement and ongoing support from the FEO will be necessary. At times, all parents can feel inadequate, out of their depth and stressed. Some parents may need and want help and support, especially when their situation is compounded by poverty, poor housing and other problems.

Home visits

For families who find it difficult to participate in opportunities to meet at school, home visits may provide the best solution. Parents are likely to feel more relaxed in their own home, and talking on a one-to-one basis without feeling rushed can help to develop a relationship and build trust. Following a successful home visit, parents often feel more confident in approaching the FEO about any concerns and are also more likely to engage in school events.

Home visits allow the FEO greater knowledge about the family, their aspirations and needs. Not only does this help to break down any stereotypes or misconceptions about a family, but having more in-depth knowledge about a student's home and family situation also enables the FEO to better relate to the student. This is particularly useful in cases where there may be concerns about behaviour or absenteeism. Home visits also provide an opportunity for the FEO to model positive interaction, encouraging parents and students to engage through games and to support homework. The FEO can also work with parents to think about how they manage certain aspects of behaviour at home and plan strategies that can be used both at home and at school.

It is recommended that the school has a Lone Worker Policy in place, designed to ensure the safety of staff who at times work on their own and/or off the school site.

Organising a home visit

An introductory letter is usually sent to all parents regarding information and the arrangement of a home visit, outlining the purpose of the visit and explaining that the FEO will contact them by phone to organise an appointment.

Once a date and time has been arranged, a reminder is sent to confirm the visit with the family a day or two beforehand – by letter, phone call, email or text. Visiting a child/family at home can be useful in a variety of situations. For example:

- A home visit is often arranged with the families of children about to start school.
- It is helpful to meet the families of children (of any age) before you start working with them, particularly if you are new to the school.
- There may be an area of concern that needs to be discussed and this cannot be done at school.
- The child is currently not attending school (e.g. because of illness).

How to keep the visit relaxed

- Make sure both the child and parents have an opportunity to ask questions or share concerns.
- Although documentation will need to be completed, organise the meeting so that it doesn't turn into an interrogation, firing a series of questions at the family. Instead, try to engage the child and family in conversation to draw out the information more informally. For example, if the child is playing with a particular toy, let this lead to a conversation about their interests, likes and dislikes. Or, if there is a family photograph on display, ask the child about any brothers/sisters or other family members. The effectiveness of eliciting information in this way will very much depend on the age of the child and the child's and/or family's response. Share your own experiences so that you come across as a 'normal' human being, not just a member of staff.
- Ask the child what they are most looking forward to about school and why, and any concerns they have so you can put their mind at ease.
- Although professionalism should always be maintained, it is very important to be relaxed and to put the family at ease so they are comfortable talking.
- At the end of the visit, thank the family for their time and hospitality, and remind them how they can contact the school for further information. Finish with a comment addressed directly to the child about how much the school is looking forward to their start at school.

Unit 4: Engaging all parents

Parent engagement is an important factor in the success of student learning, attendance, behaviour and well-being. For these reasons, increasing family engagement is an important factor for schools, but if schools want to achieve this, more opportunities and support are needed to encourage sustained engagement with parents and families. Schools that have been successful in engaging parents and other family members have implemented a variety of strategies at various levels of creativity. One such strategy is ensuring that the mindset of all school staff is one that believes in parent engagement; such a partnership can make a significant difference to student achievement. Every single parent can make a contribution to their child's learning and to the school as a whole, and therefore recognition must be given to all forms of family engagement. This unit looks at different ways to engage all parents; for more specialised interventions, see relevant unit(s).

> Family-based support is one of the most significant contributors to children's continued success in the education system, particularly during periods of educational transition.
>
> (Harris and Goodall 2009)

Venues and times

In order to engage with parents, schools need to be flexible about venue and times. For some parents, school is a daunting place, based on their own experiences as students, so take the school venue out of the equation and hold the event off site – for example, a local cafe, library, leisure centre. By keeping parents in their comfort zone, they are more likely to engage. Providing flexibility around time is also key, especially for working parents, so offer meeting times first thing in the morning when the parent drops off their child or offer a late evening once a month.

Communication

Communicating information to parents in a timely and meaningful way about their child's education, achievements and well-being allows parents to build their involvement and partnership with the school as well as support their child at home. Flexible school communication systems will help to meet the needs of all parents, especially those who are hard to reach.

It is also important that schools have a robust and timely complaints procedure in order to deal efficiently and effectively with parents who are unhappy regarding an aspect of school. In order to maintain positive relationships, issues must be dealt with in a professional way.

To ensure effective communication, the parent's preferred method of communication needs to be used and developed to allow a multifaceted approach (see 'Parent needs assessment', p. 19), so that they:

- can access information when needed via technology;
- are kept up to date with relevant information;
- gain an understanding of their child's learning;
- have opportunities to get involved with school life;
- feel empowered to support their child's learning at home;
- develop improved relationships with school staff and teachers;
- make more effective use of face-to-face time with teachers.

Some of the many forms of communication schools can use to achieve these aims are detailed in the list below and then considered in more detail.

Face-to-face	Text
Parent champions	Email
Telephone	Website
Newsletter	Facebook
Letter (general and personalised)	Twitter
Local press	YouTube
Invitations	Apps
Postcards	Blog
Notice boards	Skype
	Banners

Face-to-face

Face-to-face communication is crucial to establish trusting relationships with parents. It is a perfect opportunity to discuss the student's successes and areas where they need more support, as well as nipping potential complaints and/or grievances in the bud.

Telephone

As many parents now own a mobile phone, contacting them via a phone call is a simple way to keep them updated and involved. If parents haven't responded to an invitation to an event, then give them a call so that they know you are aware and that you care. A quick call could also encourage those who are hesitant.

Positive phone call home

Contact parents on a regular basis – say, once every two weeks – with a positive message about their child. Select two or three students each time and look for something they have done that has required effort. Keep a record of every phone call to ensure that all students have at least two or three phone calls home a year. Record the phone calls, listing the positive message, the parent's name and any other relevant information.

Parents will feel more involved and more likely to pick up the phone if they receive more positive phone calls than negative ones. Reinforce the effort their child has made in a particular subject area or just generally. Having the child in the same room when the call is being made helps to reinforce what they have achieved and also gives the parent an opportunity to have a quick chat with their child and to reinforce the positive message.

Google Voice

It is never advisable to give your personal mobile number to parents, but with a Google Voice number, linked to your own mobile phone, you can receive a call from a parent without them knowing your personal number. Also, it's a free service.

Newsletter

Newsletters can be printed on paper or sent electronically or both. The newsletter needs to be designed to provide relevant information, serve as a reminder of upcoming events and connect with parents. It is good practice for newsletters to be delivered on a set day, either on a weekly or monthly basis, so that parents will be expecting them. Below are a few suggestions for what to include in a newsletter:

- information about upcoming events, activities and meetings;
- gentle reminders about key events taking place that month;
- celebration of successes of the students, parents, staff or school in general;
- a top tips section which looks at a different theme every week/month (e.g. healthy eating, helping your child with their homework);
- links to interesting articles;
- an update on behaviour/attendance and expectations;
- a quiz/competition;
- practical tips on how parents can support their child's learning at home;
- requests for feedback regarding what parents themselves would like in the newsletter.

When writing the newsletter, consider the following:

- Use headings so that parents can easily locate the information.
- Be brief and to the point, with links to additional information if parents require more.
- Use a friendly and engaging tone.
- Consider parents whose second language is English.
- Include illustrations and photos.
- Put a 'call to action' (e.g. 'Put me on your fridge') which will help to remind parents of key dates, events etc. as it will be in easy access.

To increase the number of parents who read the newsletter, consider the following ideas:

- Print the newsletter on coloured paper (see 'What's in it for me?' on p. 86).
- Invite parents to answer questions, tear off the answer sheet and return to the school to be placed in a raffle draw to win prizes. The answers to the questions can be found in the content of the newsletter.
- Make newsletters letters available in different languages to engage ethnic minority groups.
- Survey parents' opinion of newsletters and make changes accordingly.
- Make the newsletter available as an app; when clicked on, the headteacher is seen reading out the content.
- Put the newsletter online.

Letters

Letters, like newsletters, are a simple way to communicate with parents. They can be sent weekly, monthly or whenever needed. In order to ensure parents read the letter, consider the following:

- Print the letter on coloured paper.
- Survey parents' opinion of letters and make changes accordingly.
- Make letters available in different languages to engage ethnic minority groups.
- Make the letter available as an app; when clicked on, the head teacher is seen reading out the content.
- Put a 'call to action' (e.g. 'Put me on your fridge') which will be an easy-access way to help remind parents of key dates and events.

Smart technology – smart schools

Using technology to communicate with parents means they can access information quickly and provide a prompt response if needed. Depending on the platform, schools can share videos, photos, presentations, forms and other documentation in a timely fashion.

Text

Texting parents is not only a convenient way to communicate but it is also highly likely that parents will read the text regardless of their level of literacy. There are many platforms for schools which provide a texting system for sending bulk texts – for example, www.remind.com.

Many business services send texts to remind customers about things they are likely to forget – for example, dental appointments. Research shows that text reminders can improve no-shows by around 30–40 per cent. Below are some of the benefits of sending a reminder text:

- reduces the parent no-show rate;
- produces more timely arrivals so that events can be kept on schedule;

- provides updates on opening and closing times;
- is cost-effective;
- is able to reach parents on evenings and weekends;
- has a high response rate;
- is able to inform parents immediately if an event is cancelled.

Email

Emails provide an excellent way to keep parents up to date, although the written word can sometimes be misinterpreted and cause a negative response with parents. If the communication is of a sensitive nature, it is always advisable to make a phone call first with an email follow-up. Here are some suggestion when writing emails to parents:

- Keep emails short and to the point.
- Don't use jargon.
- Where possible, personalise the email so that it engages the recipient.
- End with a 'call to action' – for example, 'Have you booked your time slot for our Parents' Evening on 24 May 2016?'
- Consider a consistent, friendly sign-off – for example, 'Best regards', 'Kind regards', 'Best wishes' or 'Yours sincerely'.
- Include on all emails a 'signature'. This can be created in the admin section of the email account and can include:
    - name and position of person sending the email
    - school name
    - address
    - telephone number
    - email
    - website
    - social media addresses
    - opening and closing times of the school
    - link to an event coming up.

Updating email addresses

For emails to be effective, email addresses must be kept up to date. Request regular email address updates from parents at key events, via text etc. Encourage teachers to ask students to notify the school of any change in their parents' email address. Inform students that in order for their parent to receive email updates or fun app communications (e.g. https://tellagami.com) an up-to-date email needs to be submitted.

School website

The school website is an accessible and invaluable form of communication for parents, providing that it is updated and monitored. The design of the website needs to provide easy access to:

- how to report your child's absence;
- contact information;
- school opening and closing times;
- out-of-hours emergency contacts;
- staff names, year group and job roles;
- school policies;
- calendar of events;
- school brochure;
- curriculum plans;
- transition information;
- homework guidance;
- uniform and where to buy;
- relevant forms to download (e.g. permission slips);
- newsletters;
- a section for feedback;
- awards the school has won;
- students' artwork and success stories.

It is not advisable to post pictures of students or their full names.

Social media

Social media platforms have made communication between home and school more efficient, and improved communication in both quantity and quality by keeping parents up-to-date regarding key events, interesting articles, homework assignments, etc. It is advisable when using platforms that the school has an 'acceptable use' policy for staff, parents and students, making everyone aware of what's appropriate to post. It is important that schools communicate through the channels parents are using every day, such as Twitter, Facebook, Instagram, Pinterest, blogs. It is important that posts develop a two-way conversation or 'call to action' for parents. Below are a few suggestions on using social media to engage parents:

- Post homework assignments and projects.
- Celebrate and showcase students' achievements.
- Signpost to relevant information and contacts.
- Give information about project deadlines.
- Inform parents of school news.
- Send reminders of key events and meetings.
- Conduct polls to gauge feedback.
- Ask questions to get feedback and comments.
- Post videos of what the children are learning in class.
- Give top tips on how to talk to your child.
- Set up a Facebook group to share resources (e.g. to help students with revision).
- Set up Twitter subject or year group accounts to provide information about homework assignments, reminders, top tips, etc.

Social media management

Posting on social media platforms such as Twitter and Facebook can be time-consuming – according to some analysts, organisations should be tweeting a minimum of three times a day and posting on Facebook five times a week. To ensure consistency and engagement on these platforms, using social media management tools can be of great benefit. The most popular of these are Hootsuite, Buffer, IFTTT, SocialOomph.

Pinterest

Pinterest is a great way to connect school staff and parents via a visual bookmarking application which allows users to discover and save creative ideas in a variety of different categories (e.g. homework). Everyone can follow one another and even build boards together and share ideas. Go to https://uk.pinterest.com/nsmtraining for lots of ideas on engaging families.

Instagram

This platform provides a 'show not tell' way of sharing photos. Like other social media, a group can be formed using hashtags. This provides a great communication tool for your visual learner as it is all done through photos and videos. This platform can be used in so many different ways to engage parents. Here are a few suggestions:

- Create a school brochure.
- Display a notice board celebrating student/parent achievements.
- Create a book club showing parents' and students' favourite books to encourage others to read.
- Show students' work.
- Select a student of the week to upload photos showing what they did in a week.
- Run a competition such as 'guess the object'. Ask students/parents to upload an obscure photo of an object and whoever guesses it correctly wins a prize. This encourages creativity in looking at objects around us in a different way.

Google Drive

Google Drive is a free service and a productive and cost-effective way to work with parents regarding their child's education. The good thing about Google Drive is that parents don't have to pay for Microsoft Office in order to read documents that have been sent to them. Uploaded information can be downloaded on to smartphones and tablets as well as computers. Below are a few suggestions on what to upload on to the platform:
Create:

- contact forms for parents to add their details to be included in a database;
- registration forms for parents to sign up to key events;
- school trip forms;
- behaviour and attendance updates for parents.

Share:

- back-to-school information;
- class newsletters;
- homework assignments;
- class/subject group work;
- student presentations;
- parent workshop content via video or audio.

Blog

Many schools are now writing blogs to keep parents updated. Blogs are also a great way to get parents involved in the classroom so that they feel part of the learning experience without having to be there physically. Blogs are effective when they are written in a practical way and as if the writer is having a conversation with the reader. This way, opinions can be expressed to generate conversations. Make use of photos, videos and links to further support or additional information. Below are a few suggestions:

- Inform parents about homework assignments and other home projects.
- Post homework submission dates.
- Ask students to upload photos and videos to convey what they have been learning.
- Ask questions to help engage parents in the learning process and ask for feedback.
- Hold a 'Student of the Week' to celebrate that child's achievements. (Make sure a list is kept so that every student is included at some point.)

Skype

Skype allows parents to have a face-to-face conversation with a member of staff or be a part of workshops and/or classroom-based activities without having to physically be at the school. This is an ideal communication tool for parents who work in the armed forces and for engaging grandparents who live in different locations. It is advisable that the school implements a policy to ensure the safety of staff.

Apps

Apps provide a wide range of ways to engage with parents, not only to help support their child in learning but also to provide more effective communication with the school without physically being there. Apps can provide parents with:

- updates on school news;
- easy access to school policies;
- school calendar and reminders of events and meetings;
- directions in and maps of the school;
- homework reminders;
- updates on attendance and behaviour;

- learning programmes on different subjects;
- information about transport links to get to school;
- translation services;
- up-to-date information about their child's learning;
- information to enable parents to be more engaged with their child's learning.

Survey

Not only is setting up a systematic process to seek parents' feedback a great way to assess what's working well and what needs to be improved on, it also gives parents a voice and makes them feel more involved in school life. There are many ways to survey parents. Below are a few examples.

Suggestion box

Using a suggestion box can help a school understand parents' views. If the same suggestion appears several times, it highlights an area where changes might be made. As with everything, of course, a suggestion box only works if parents use it, so publicise the importance of the box in newsletters as well as on a TV screen in the foyer area, with information to help guide parents to use it. Place the box in an accessible and visible area such as next to the signing-in book.

Tell us about yourself

It's always a good idea to send out surveys to parents to assess their needs and also establish how they can contribute to school life. Find out what they are interested in – what do they want to know or be able to do? A survey could include the following.

I'd like to . . .

- help set up and maintain a community garden;
- help choreograph the school play;
- paint a mural in the school hall;
- talk to a class about being a sanctuary for injured hedgehogs;
- help design and build a role-play area (e.g. a Viking ship);
- coach a football/rugby/netball team.

Things I like to do – Things I don't like to do

Ask parents to complete a survey listing in one column what they like to do and in the other column what they don't like to do. This provides a great source of information so that school can contact a parent to ask if they'd volunteer for something they like to do.

You said – We did

When parents have completed surveys and their feedback has been analysed, pick a handful of suggestions they have made, create a 'You said – We did' display board in the reception area or a board on the school website. Write each suggestion in turn under 'You said' and then under 'We did' write what the school has done to address it, for example:

> You said . . . You found it hard to find out how to give us feedback.
> We did . . . We introduced our new Comments & Complaints section on the website.

This process provides a great motivator for parents as they can see their feedback has been noted, responded to and implemented.

Incentives for handing in surveys/questionnaires

Surveys and questionnaires provide invaluable information, but only if they are completed and returned. Below are a few suggestions on how to achieve this:

- Offer prizes for those who return the survey/questionnaire.
- Hand out surveys/questionnaires to a captive audience. For example, while parents are waiting for the school performance to start, give them a questionnaire with a printed raffle ticket attached. When the questionnaire is completed, they can place it in the box and at the end of the performance there will be a raffle draw to win the prizes listed on the ticket.
- Ask students to take the survey/questionnaire home and encourage a parent to complete it. When it's returned to school, they are rewarded with ten house points.
- During parents' evening when parents are waiting or just as they are about to leave, guide them towards a computer to complete an online questionnaire.
- Remember to provide pens and pencils as well as staff on hand to assist any parents who have a low literacy level.

Transitions

Transition is always about change, not just for the students but also for the parents. Surveys have shown that students around this time benefit from more contact with the school for support and information. It is also a key time for a school to form trusting relationships with new parents which will benefit the engagement role of the school. Visiting their child's new place of learning for the first time can be daunting for any parent, so take the stress away in the following ways:

- Use different forms of communication to share information and address parental concerns and needs.
- Invite parents to an informal information evening where they can meet the staff, look around the school and ask questions.
- Create a worry box for parents to share concerns or ask questions. Make this available online as well as a physical box in the reception area.
- Send parents a link to view photos and information about members of staff.
- Allocate a key member of staff to each parent as a point of contact.
- Offer opportunities for the parent to join their child in class so that they can experience what their child is learning.

- Provide parents with links to other professionals they may need to access such as translators or health professionals.
- Allocate a morning a week where parents can drop off their child and stay to talk to other parents.
- Provide parents with top tips on helping to support their child with the transition.
- Help parents prepare their child before attending school by establishing good routines (e.g. bedtime).

Secondary schools

It is well documented that a parent's engagement often decreases when their child goes to secondary school. According to Cotton and Wikelund (1989), there are several possible reasons for the lack of parental engagement at secondary school, including the following:

- Secondary schools tend to be larger and further from home.
- The curriculum is more sophisticated.
- Students have more than one teacher.
- Parents of older students are more likely to be in full-time employment.
- Children are beginning to establish a sense of separation from their parents.

Another possible reason could be that parents are not clear about what is expected of them in school. School staff need to be very clear about how they'd like parents to engage – and how staff will engage, for example:

- checking homework and making sure it is handed in on time;
- supporting their child though course selection;
- attending key meetings such as parents' evenings;
- showing an interest and providing home learning support;
- providing support to help with their child's revision;
- providing guidance to enable parents to support learning at home;
- providing information regarding about what their child is studying;
- providing schedules for upcoming exams.

School brochure

The school brochure contains lots of information about the child's new school as well as information for the parents to help prepare their child for the transition process. To address any further concerns, the brochure can be written by parents for parents by forming a focus group and collecting thoughts from parents about what information would be helpful and relevant to them. Remind parents to ask questions if they need further information or assistance.

Welcome pack for new parents

As well as providing new parents with the school brochure (ensure it is available in multiple languages), why not create a welcome pack containing the following:

- the school brochure;
- a copy of the home-school agreement;
- a calendar of events;
- a list of after-school clubs;
- a list of activities taking place within the area;
- details about the family drop-in centre;
- related home-school activities such as the Family Values Scheme (see Unit 10);
- guidance about how to become a school volunteer, parent governor, member of the parent teacher association, etc.;
- a request for feedback from parents via surveys to continue to revise and improve the handbook;
- induction kit (see below).

Induction kit

An induction kit can be created by parents, providing easy-to-use guidance about the transition process – for example, a top-tips booklet listing the things parents want to know but may be too shy to ask. A checklist of everything your child needs when attending school could also be included.

Welcome letter

Before the beginning of the school year, send home a letter to parents not only to welcome them but also giving information to help get their child ready for the new year. This information can include:

- list of school uniform required;
- equipment needed for classes;
- contact information for form teacher;
- school start and finish times;
- information about the back-to-school night (see below).

Back-to-school night

Invite parents and students to a back-to-school night at the beginning of the school year. This provides a great opportunity for parents to meet their child's class teacher and have a guided tour of the school. It is also the night that sets the tone for your entire year with the parents of your new students. Below are some ideas for creating a successful evening:

Invitations

Make invitations to parents warm and welcoming. Consider the following:

- *Student-created invitations* – get students to design a personal invitation addressed to a family member(s).

- *Phone call home* – this is a great way to establish the teacher–parent relationship; even if the parent doesn't pick up, a voice message can be left.
- *Welcome brochure* – create a brochure listing the timetable of the event, the location and an overview of the evening. The brochure can also include information being shared by the teacher during the evening.
- *E-invitations* – choose an online app such as Invite Shop or Tellagami to create an invitation and send it via email or text.
- *Bilingual invitations* – for parents whose second language is English, make sure invitations are written in their first language.
- *Video invitations* – be creative and work with students to create a short sketch involving an invitation, then film it and send it via email or text.
- *Postcard invitations* – these make a great invitation, whether in paper format or using an app such as PhotoCard.

Organisation

- *Sign-in sheets* – place sign-in sheets on every table to avoid long queues and delayed activities.
- *The classroom environment* – ensure the classrooms are tidy, with students' work displayed.
- *Teacher presentation* – plan and practise the presentation so that it informs and keeps the interest of the families present.
- *Family activities* – design and organise some exciting activities for families to take part in during the evening session. Consider activities for younger as well as older siblings.

Key meetings and events

During the academic year there are many meetings and events that parents are asked to attend – for example, parents' evenings, reviews of individual education plans (IEPs). There are many different reasons that some parents don't attend. Here are some suggestions to address this:

- Vary the meeting time and venue.
- Disguise meetings and events.
- Use the grown-up method (see Unit 8).
- Use positive reinforcements.
- Offer a babysitting service.
- Consider the duration and frequency of meetings and events.
- Combine meetings with other school events.
- Advertise well.

Meeting times and venues

Surveys are one way to discover what times best suit your parents to ensure improved attendance. Remember, meetings don't have to be face-to-face and they don't have to take place in school. Be creative and offer variety. Meetings can take place in any of the following:

- cafe or pub
- football club
- library
- supermarket
- children's centre
- health and fitness club.

Auxiliary staff

When the school has decided on a calendar of activities and events for parents, it is important the information is shared with the school's auxiliary staff, especially if parents are accessing school in the evening or early morning. Acknowledging and positively reinforcing staff will go a long way.

Develop virtual partnerships

Working parents naturally find that work schedules sometimes prevent them from engaging at their child's school and community. Finding creative and innovative ways to engage can therefore provide many benefits. Below are a few examples:

- Be flexible with venues and meeting times. Provide appointments before 8 a.m. and after 5.30 p.m.
- Run twilight meetings, events and activities.
- Keep meetings short, concise and to the point.
- Allow children at meetings, either by providing childcare facilities or activities and/or resources to entertain them.
- Hold weekend fun events that all family members can come along to.
- Don't rely on parents physically being at the school – consider, for example, video conferencing, instant messaging, video diaries, online forums, online polling, etc.
- Create learning materials for home – for example, the Family Values Scheme (see Unit 10).
- Form relationships with local businesses and send information to parents via notice boards.
- Partner with local businesses to support lunchtime focus group meetings and workshops arranged by the school for parents.

Positive reinforcements

It is a good way forward for the school to have in place a policy on how to positively reinforce parents. This ensures consistency and fairness across the board as well as recognising and acknowledging the support given by parents in helping with their child's education. A simple 'Thank you' can go a long way towards strengthening parents' self-confidence and self-belief and help to build trusting and respectful relationships. Below are a few examples of positive reinforcements.

Time credits

'Spice Time Credits' are a wonderful way of rewarding parents. Parents can be thanked with these credits for contributing time to their school or community. They then 'spend' time credits to access events, training and leisure services or to thank others in turn. Schools and local community groups identify current and new opportunities for people to give their time. The new opportunities are based on the interests, skills and availability of parents, and are enabled and supported by school and community services. Public, community and private organisations identify ways for people to spend time credits in their services or at events. This can be 'spare capacity' at theatres or swimming pools, for example, or for community services as a way of recognising and thanking people for the contributions they have made (trips for young people on free school meals become trips for young people who have contributed). Spice spend brochures include a wide range of community organisations as well as higher-profile opportunities such as the Barbican and Tower of London.

Earn time credits:

- attending a school activity with your child;
- helping at an after-school event;
- attending or setting up a parent council within the school;
- litter picking in the park.

Spend time credits:

- at the school where you earned them;
- on other local activities and opportunities;
- by giving them to someone as a thank you;
- anywhere across the UK network.

> Using Time Credits at Baden Powell Primary School has benefited the school community immensely. Parents feel more appreciated when they give their time to organising school events, such as the fayre and disco. We are able to say thank you with the credits – we are even paying Santa Claus with Time Credits! We use the Time Credits to enhance intergenerational activities and the amount of families that have been involved in activities has increased. For example, since September, attendance at homework clubs has soared from 5 to 35. Spending opportunities have given families a sense of pride and the children have had big smiles when they were able to pay for the disco knowing they had worked as a family to gain the credits.
>
> Emma Williams, Parental Engagement Teacher at Baden Powell Primary School

Free tickets

Using a school loyalty card system, offering parents free or reduced-price tickets to activities or events, can be a positive incentive.

Raffle tickets

Raffle tickets are a great way to reward parents. They don't necessarily have to be used for a prize draw, but instead can be used as tokens which can be collected and traded in for something desirable – for example, an extra ticket for the end-of-year concert.

Celebration area

Create a family celebration board in the reception area, where parents' achievements, success stories, team wins and talents can be displayed and celebrated by all. Include photos, newspaper articles, trophies, etc.

Submit application

Enter parents' achievements, successes and projects into local, regional, national and even international awards.

Babysitting service

It is sometimes difficult for parents to attend meetings or events if they have very young children; offering a free babysitting service within school is key. Working parents who have paid for childcare provision during the day may be reluctant to do so again in the evening, so this type of service in school will be very welcomed.

Sticker advertising approach

On the day of a key meeting/event, give each student a sticker to wear before they leave school to remind parents. The sticker can say something like 'Parents Evening Tonight at 4 p.m.'

Events

Consider whether the events you organise support the education and welfare of the students. Below are some suggestions.

Don't stop moving

Hold a fitness club once a week after school.

Mega challenge events

Introduce mega challenges once every month. These can include:

- an obstacle course;
- board game challenge;

- treasure hunt – using map-reading skills;
- a fashion show – create an outfit from recycled materials;
- create a family crest – using paint, paper, card, glitter, etc.;
- kite making – using ICT to establish a design, making and flying the kite.

Coffee mornings

Coffee mornings can be about more than just coffee:

- book mornings related to World Book Day;
- students serve their mums and dads.

Family night

Fun ways of getting parents and children involved together might include:

- Italian night;
- race night;
- film night;
- art workshop;
- picnics.

Assemblies

Different kinds of assembly might include:

- a weekly celebration assembly or reward assemblies;
- student leadership assemblies;
- a class assembly every half-term;
- children performing and hosting events for their parents.

Fundraising

Ideas for fundraising might include:

- collaborative parent and child competitions;
- involvement in charity events;
- fundraising activities for specific trips and equipment.

Grandparents' days

Create a grandparents' day in the school or community and ask students' grandparents to attend. Put on food and refreshments and organise activities such as knitting, creating a family tree, baking.

Enterprise day

Ideas include:

- student-led events to bring in the parents;
- a community fun day;
- open afternoons to see the school at work and play.

Volunteering

There are many volunteering opportunities for parents, including:

- helping in the classroom;
- helping at seasonal fairs;
- collecting vouchers for schools from local supermarkets and petrol stations;
- helping to organise a fundraising event;
- being a playground supervisor;
- being a school/class trip helper;
- organising and/or assisting after-school clubs (e.g. chess);
- coaching the school football or netball team;
- participating in the walking bus scheme;
- creating costumes for school performances.

Healthy eating

Include parents in:

- healthy snack preparation;
- a lunchtime mother's day or father's day meal.

Below is an example of engaging families in healthy eating.

Communities First healthy lunchbox session for families at Penygraig Junior School

Penygraig Junior School in South Wales wanted to increase the number of parent helpers who engage with the school and to give the opportunity to learn about healthy choices when preparing their children's lunchboxes. Due to the high number of unhealthy packed lunches, the school also wanted to focus on educating children and family members on the amounts of sugar, salt, fat, etc. in everyday lunch items. The school decided to organise an event with the support of Communities First, delivering a range of other related sessions.

Organisation of event

Mrs Allison Carter, the school's family engagement staff member, arranged a meeting with Communities First staff to see if they were in a position to run any sessions for the school, as their aims are the same as ours but out in the community. They were keen to do so, and offered many more opportunities to the school, providing they could engage the parents.

The school decided to get the parents through the door by inviting them to a coffee morning. During this relaxed session the parents were informed that the event theme was healthy lunchboxes/healthy eating, followed by games, quizzes and activities that they could participate in with their children. Prizes were also offered to the children.

The school made a decision not to inform parents at the beginning that the event was being run by Communities First. It was thought that some of the parents would choose not to attend if they associated Communities First with these other activities.

Mrs Carter prepared a letter and a colourful party invitation with an RSVP for the children to take home. Children were told that they could only come to the 'party' if they brought a grown-up to school with them. Children were encouraged to go home and nag their parents to come! Refreshments and healthy snacks for the parents and children were organised out of the school budget. All other resources, including ingredients for the 'make a healthy wrap for lunch' activity were provided by Communities First out of their budget.

Communities First staff ran the whole session, and Mrs Carter and another staff member attended and encouraged/praised the participation of the parents and children. There were family games in the hall, 'warm-up' quizzes on healthy eating and games to guess the amount of sugar in popular children's drinks and snacks. Ideas for healthy alternatives were provided. The children and their families were encouraged to try new healthy foods when choosing their ingredients to make a healthy tortilla wrap for lunch. There was a giant 'Eat Well plate' where children had to place a variety of foods in the correct sections. All families were given a folder to take home containing games, quizzes and activities for the children, and some simple and healthy recipes for the adults. All children were given a free 'Change 4 Life' swim bag, water bottle and stickers.

Impact

- The school invited the parents of two classes to this event. There are 56 children in these two classes. Twenty-five parents/grandparents attended so nearly 50 per cent of the children were able to attend with an adult. This was the highest percentage the school has ever had to an event, excluding Christmas/Summer whole-school productions.
- Children and family members were keen to have refreshments together in the school environment. Overall, they were pleased with the event and enjoyed interacting with their children and other parents in a relaxed environment.

- The children liked trying healthy snacks that they had not tasted before. The children and the adults all felt that they had learnt at least one new thing about healthy eating and came up with some good healthy alternatives for lunchbox fillings.
- No one complained about not being told beforehand that Communities First would be running the event, even though they were asked to complete Communities First registration forms.
- Adults participated in all of the activities with enthusiasm, even the silly games in the hall.
- Feedback was very positive and many parents, after hearing what else Communities First could offer, said they would like to attend an after-school cooking club with their child. This is something that Communities First are able to offer us and we are considering for the future.
- The event was so successful that the school is running it again. This time the school has decided to run two separate events – one per class over two consecutive days, as with over 50 adults and children in attendance last time it was a little crowded in the space available for the event.
- Some parents who attended the event with their children last time are attending again this month as they have younger children in the school.

Allison Carter, Learning Support Assistant and Family Engagement, Penygraig
Junior School

Unit 5: Engaging dads

Importance of engaging dads

Fathers play an important role in their children's education. There is significant research showing that involving fathers in their children's education has many positive outcomes on children's intellectual development, social competence and emotional well-being (Clark 2009; Geddes 2008). According to Potter *et al.* (2012), fathers need to be involved in their children's learning and development right from early years schooling. However, some fathers encounter barriers to engagement, for example:

- work commitments;
- separated fathers who do not regularly see their child;
- a lack of awareness of services offered;
- a lack of organisational support;
- concerns over the content of the services;
- fathers who see school involvement as the mother's responsibility;
- past poor learning experiences discouraging fathers' commitment;
- the discounting of fathers' own sociocultural experiences and knowledge leading to disengagement.

Although finding ways of engaging fathers, grandfathers and male carers can be particularly challenging, schools need to make sure that this is achieved as the impact of fathers and male role models on children's educational, social and emotional development is very important. Time and planning for this area are key to achieving the best results. Here are a few suggestions:

- Review all printed material including information online to reference 'dads' or 'fathers'. Use these terms rather than the word 'parents'. Evidence suggests that dads are unlikely to assume the word 'parents' means them, so rephrasing will increase the likelihood of their attendance.
- Make sure that promotional materials about your school contain photos/pictures of dads. Use posters with interesting images and messages relevant to males. Use cartoons, captions and eye-catching headlines.

- Ask staff to use the terms 'mums, dads and carers' so that dads are not forgotten or made to feel excluded or marginalised.
- Understand the culture of 'modern fatherhood'. Use catchy phrases (e.g. dads and lads, just for men, fathers' day, fathers' play).
- During staff meetings ask each member to come up with one effective way to engage dads. Use the Disney model on p. 16.
- Consider the following terms when engaging male family members:
  - biological father
  - father figure
  - stepfather
  - foster dad
  - granddad
  - uncle
  - role model
  - brother.

Communication

Communication system

It is important to have a well-thought-out communication system for dads so that they are included in all correspondence, regardless of whether they are separated or not.

Direct communication

Communicate directly with dads and ask for work/home details in order to send emails, letters, etc. Consider how you can best meet their needs and communicate in 'male-friendly' ways. Keep messages short. Talk about 'objects and things' rather than 'people and feelings'. Use strong positive language such as 'results', 'success' and 'achievement.'

Advertise, advertise

Consider advertising school events in places dads go to or in newspapers/magazines they read. For example, put posters in pubs, health centres, gyms, toilets, places of work and local shops.

Use technology

Increase your use of new technologies. Use more text messaging, blogs, Facebook, online polling. Use more visuals, videos, DVD clips.

The 'P' word

Events advertised for 'parents' tend to attract mothers, so address letters to dads, and try other media too: text messages, emails or a website. Are there other organisations that can help you reach dads – libraries, schools, sports clubs, community groups or even a local employer?

Dad's page

Create a specific page for dads on the school website. Post upcoming activities, information on how to help your child with reading, how they can volunteer within the school, DVD clips, testimonials from other dads, etc.

Venues and times

Some fathers may feel they don't have a role at the school as most activities tend to be held during the school day. Flexibility regarding venue and times is therefore important. Schools need to be flexible about meeting times to ensure that working dads are included. Consider venues such as football clubs, pub function rooms and Internet cafes. Remember that first impressions are vital. If your venue is welcoming and encourages dads to get involved, they will know the service is for them.

Marketing to fathers

The dad audit

To establish the level of dad involvement within your school, conduct an audit for a week to find out how many males and females drop off and collect their child. Analyse the results and consider what your school can do to improve the engagement of dads.

Solution finders

Approach dads in terms of solution finders by setting them challenges with their child – for example, a den-building evening. Engage them as solution finders by inviting them to be part of the school improvement team. Ask fathers for their advice on factors such as website content, design, publicity, recruitment, themes, timing and venue.

Questionnaire

Asking dads what they want is the best place to start. This can be achieved by devising a short questionnaire. Select questions and word in a dad-friendly way. Include questions such as:

- What is the best time for you to take part in school activities and/or meet with staff?
- How would you like the school to keep you up to date with your child's progress?
- What activities would you like the school to offer for you and your child?
- How would you like the school to involve and engage with you?
- In what way would you like to volunteer within the school?
- What skills can you share within the school?

Inspiring dads

Create a display board in the school foyer with photos of dads getting involved with school. Add captions underneath each photo saying why they got involved and what they got out of it. This can also be coupled with famous dads in sport and film, with quotes regarding their children's development and education.

Use a dad-friendly hook

A great way to get most dads' attention is through sport, whether participating or just being a spectator, particularly (although not exclusively) football. This doesn't have to take place within the school but instead could be held at a sports arena or football ground where a tour of the grounds at the end of the activity could prove to be a big hit.

It's all in the name

Understand the culture of 'modern fatherhood'. Use catchy phrases to attract more dads:

- Dads and lads
- Who let the dads out?
- Just for men
- Fathers' day
- Fathers' play
- DUG (dads, uncles, granddads)
- Blokes on board
- FUDGE (friends, uncles, dads, grandpas, etc.)
- Boys to men
- Superdads
- Dads included
- #howtodad
- Dad's army
- Proud pappas.

Mum knows best

In order to engage more dads in school, ask the mums as they normally act as gatekeepers for their child's education and will often know what will motivate the dads to get involved. Set up a focus group with a select group of mums and encourage them to suggest innovative ways to get dads involved - use the Disney model on p. 16.

Supporting learning

Dadanory

Jackanory was a long-running BBC children's television series that was designed to stimulate an interest in reading. Why not rename the popular TV series *Dadanory* to encourage dads to read to their child at home? Open up the activity by suggesting to dads they can record the story they read and upload it on to the school website to encourage other dads to take part. They can get lots of ideas by watching and listening to stories on the Jackanory Junior section of the CBeebies website.

Storytelling workshops

Advertise a storytelling workshop and invite a local author to provide dads with top tips and offer advice on how to read with children at home.

Beer and books

Organise a reading group for dads in the local pub or cafe where they can meet once a month to discuss a book they are reading and books they are reading with their child. This is a great opportunity for key staff to form good working relationships with dads. Things to consider when setting up a book club:

- *Number of dads*. A good number is around 8–10 to generate discussion.
- *Frequency*. Once a month is an ideal time frame as it gives everyone the opportunity to have read something.
- *Venue*. Somewhere quiet but familiar – for example, a pub or cafe.
- *Book selection*. Encourage dads to pick a book in turn. This will not only provide variety for the group but will also instill confidence within the group.

Beyond the book

Give dads lots of examples of reading with their child which doesn't just revolve around the traditional book – for example, articles online, websites, magazines, posters, newspapers, television guides, maps.

Barber shop

Some dads with daughters may struggle when asked to do their hair in a ponytail or braids. Ask a local hairdresser or barber to provide a workshop teaching dads key skills when it comes to their child's hair. Certificates can be presented to the dads on completion.

Activities

Dads often prefer to do something rather than talk about it, so try to incorporate activities into sessions such as parents' evenings and reading workshops – for example, quizzes, interactive games, online activities, puzzles and visits from authors. It is important to note that although holding a one-off event to grab dads' attention can work well, a retention strategy needs to be implemented to ensure ongoing engagement.

Father's Day celebration evening

This is a great way to bring not only dads but other family members together. Organise fun activities with great food.

Dads into school days

If you work in a school, ask dads to come in and find out about what their children are up to all day. Consider open-house events for fathers, dads into school days, dads' breakfasts and lunches, and evenings to celebrate Father's Day.

Boys' night

Organising a boys' night gives dads and other male carers the opportunity to come into school with their child and have fun while learning new skills about how to better support learning at home. This is not only a fun evening but also provides the dads with increased confidence, skills and knowledge regarding their child's learning.

Dads 4 dinner

Invite dads to join their child for lunch in the canteen during the school day. An effective way to do this is by year group so that the appropriate members of staff can also dine with the dads and answer any questions they may have regarding their child's education and well-being. Consider using some fun names to entice dads in and theme the food accordingly:

- Dads Diner
- Fathers of the Caribbean
- Donuts with Dad
- Daddy's Day Cafe
- The Cod Father.

Business breakfasts

Invite working dads into the school for a business breakfast and provide a speaker and net-working opportunities with staff and other dads. This event could last for just 30 minutes – enough time to eat, network and enjoy listening to a speaker.

BBQ

As a fun twist, have the fathers and their children make bird houses out of wood. Set up a table with nails, hammers, scrap pieces of wood and glue. This gives the dads and kids some-thing fun to do while they wait for their food.

Compete and eat

Dads love a competition, so why not put on a 'Compete and Eat' night where food is provided in the form of curry or bacon rolls and the room is full of traditional games such as draughts, billiards, pool, chess, backgammon, etc.

Design a score board where all names are listed and invite dads to choose a game and an opponent (this can be done randomly by pulling a name out of a hat). Staff can be on hand to explain the game rules as well as participate to ensure equal numbers.

Offer male-focused prizes, rewards or incentives (e.g. football tickets, PlayStation games, outdoor activities, DVDs, health and fitness magazines) to encourage more dads to engage with the service.

Grand Prix banana race

Set up a racetrack (a length of board that can be elevated slightly at one end to create a slope for a car to roll) in a large room and supply each dad/child team with a banana and construction items needed to build a car. Give each team a set time to construct their car and information about the length of the track the cars will race on.

Three or four teams race at a time and the winner of each race is logged on a board. The winner from each race will compete against the other winners until an overall winner is announced.

Celebrate the winners (first, second and third) in true Grand Prix-style by standing on a platform and presenting with a trophy. Take loads of photos and display on a designated board in the school. Providing food is always a good option.

Seed money

For dads who are entrepreneurs, this is a great activity to stimulate productivity. Invite families to an information evening on how to participate in the 'seed money' activity. Each family is given the challenge to make their money grow to raise funds for the school. The task takes place over a three-week period and each family is given £1 to start their investment. Below are a list of entrepreneurial ideas families may want to consider:

- Club together and buy products in bulk in order to sell at a profit.
- Organise a fundraising event at the school or in the community.
- Offer a car-washing service on weekends.
- Sell tickets to a performance.

Other activities

- *Break-time games*. Open up the playground to dads after school or on weekends so that they can play and engage with their child in organised games.
- *Curry night*. Hold a curry night at the school and invite dads to sample curries as well as engage with staff about helping to improve their child's standards, behaviour, attendance, etc.

- *Master Chef*. Organise a Master Chef evening where dads learn how to cook dishes and prepare healthy meals that they can enjoy with their child.
- *Football team*. Set up a school or community football team for dads, allocate a member of staff or a local football coach to coach the team, and schedule matches with other schools and clubs in the area.
- *A Question of Sport*. After enjoying a game of football, why not hold a sports quiz based on the TV programme *A Question of Sport*?
- *Radio show*. Set up and involve dads through making radio programmes that can be podcast, put on the school website and enjoyed by all. The podcasts can include top tips, reading with your child, etc.
- *Film club*. Offer sessions for dads to learn about movie making. Lend digital video cameras and get children to make videos with their dads. Have an Oscar evening at school, including the red carpet and trophies, and invite families to watch and vote on their favourite film clip.
- *Build and create*. Hold an evening for building and creating – from the strongest, tallest tower to the biggest tent. Provide practical sessions with top tips and skill sharing.
- *Challenge Dad*. Every week/month send home a 'Challenge Dad' activity. Ask dads to produce evidence that they have completed the activity; the evidence can be displayed in the foyer area so all can see.

Volunteering opportunities

Dads under the hammer

Hold an auction event where families not only bid for items donated to the school (e.g. from local sports clubs) but also bid for dads to donate their time at home for key activities – for example, two hours of bedtime reading for their child, three hours bike-riding with their child.

Yellow Pages board

Many superstores have an area where local businesses are able to display their business card to inform local people of the services they can provide. Why not offer this concept to your dads? Have a designated board in the reception area for them to add their business card and publicise this service on your website and newsletters. Charge dads an hour of their time to help out around the school.

Ambassador dads

Ensure everyone is aware of the importance of dads and male role-models in their children's educational, social and emotional development. Select one or two dads who engage with school on a regular basis and train them up to be ambassador dads. Their role(s) can involve:

- helping to engage more dads;
- decision-making about planning activities and community involvement;
- coordinating fundraising activities and school programmes;

- publicising events taking part in school;
- providing opportunities to help and support their child;
- offering workshops.

Gardening

Set up a gardening club with dads and allocate part of the school grounds to be transformed into allotments. Here fruit and vegetables can be grown and eaten by the students and families or even sold at school fairs.

A man who can

Ask dads to offer their skills and time around the school – for example, running the BBQ at the school fete, maintaining sports equipment, helping out at sports day.

Skill swap

Ask dads to complete a questionnaire about the types of skills they can offer and the types of things they'd like to learn. Match the skills swap with members of staff and students so that everyone is learning and benefiting from each other.

Transforming classrooms

Invite dads to lend a hand in painting and transforming classrooms. This type of activity can take place during the evening and/or school holidays.

Unit 6: Engaging multicultural parents

Introduction

School engagement with multicultural parents can provide opportunities as well as cultural challenges. Creating a culturally aware partnership with parents can not only reduce cultural challenges but also develop sustainable relationships. These cultural differences may be interpreted as parents not wanting to engage with school, although in some cases parents may not be aware of the expected norms of parental engagement. According to Trumbull *et al.* (2003), some research shows that communication problems are as much about differences between parents' values and the implicit values of the school as they are about language barriers. Evidence also suggests that parents want to get involved in their child's education, particularly in decision-making, and that they respond positively where this happens (Williams and Churchill 2006). Schools must therefore communicate clearly to parents to avoid misconceptions which could conflict with cultural norms and present engagement in a variety of ways to increase uptake.

> In order for all parents to remain positive influences in their children's education at every grade level, all schools must develop and maintain effective and goal-linked programs of family and community involvement.
>
> (Hutchins *et al.* 2012)

According to Trumbull *et al.*, 'minority' parent involvement in children's schooling is a positive thing to the degree that it can result in:

- teachers' increased understanding of the families and communities children come from;
- parents' increased understanding of how schools operate;
- opportunities for a mutually forged school culture.

But until schools (meaning teachers, administrators, other personnel) understand how cultural values influence the goals and practices of childrearing, the views of education and the ways that people interact, they will not succeed in attaining the kind of 'minority' parent involvement they claim to want or in providing the best education for 'minority' students.

Culture

Parents' culture can be defined and expressed in many ways. Maschinot (2008) suggests that it is 'a shared system of meaning, which includes values, beliefs, and assumptions expressed in daily interactions of individuals within a group through a definite pattern of language, behavior, customs, attitudes, and practices'. According to Edwards *et al.* (in press), culture can also be defined as:

> a way of life, especially as it relates to the socially transmitted habits, customs, traditions, and beliefs that characterize a particular group of people at a particular time. It includes the behaviors, actions, practices, attitudes, norms and values, communications (language) patterns, traits, etiquette, spirituality, concepts of health and healing, superstitions, and institutions of a racial, ethnic, religious, or social group. It is the lens through which we look at the world.

Either way, as Trumbull and Pacheco (2005) simplistically put it, 'Our own culture is often hidden from us, and we frequently describe it as "the way things are".'

Cultural iceberg

In 1976 Edward T. Hall suggested that culture is like an iceberg in that there are two parts to culture – the visible (above the waterline) and the less visible (below the waterline). It is therefore clear from Figure 6.1 that culture has some aspects that are visible, such as dress and language, and other aspects that are less visible, such as values and beliefs.

According to Hall, the best way to understand and learn about a person's beliefs and values is to engage in their culture as it is, so that what is hidden beneath the surface becomes more apparent.

Barriers to engagement

According to Page *et al.* (2008), minority ethnic parents are likely to be disproportionately affected by barriers such as a lack of time, travelling distances, costs and language, especially when English is a second language. Other barriers for minority groups could include:

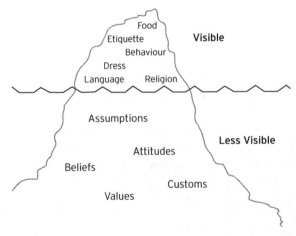

Figure 6.1 Cultural iceberg.

- cultural differences;
- disabilities;
- childcare needs;
- relocation and/or isolation;
- lack of family cohesion;
- discrimination issues;
- lack of trust;
- economic imbalances;
- lack of understanding regarding the education system;
- thinking that they don't play an important role in their child's education.

Staff training

As highlighted in Unit 2, staff training is an essential ingredient when engaging parents, and additional training around culture, diversity and understanding can significantly help when looking to engage parents from multicultural groups. Barriers to engagement may be affected by cultural issues, and by having an awareness and understanding of these, effective approaches and strategies can be implemented and guidance can be provided on how to respond to common questions and comments. A clear understanding of the school/ authority's anti-discriminatory practice is also advisable.

Cultural awareness training

Training in this area provides an understanding that we are all shaped by our cultural background, which ultimately influences our values, behaviour and beliefs. Of course, within any culture these values and beliefs can vary according to the individual. According to the National Clearinghouse for Alcohol and Drug Information (NCADI) of the Substance Abuse and Mental Health Services Administration (SAMHSA) cultural awareness training should:

- acknowledge culture as a predominant force in shaping behaviours, values and institutions;
- acknowledge and accept that cultural differences exist and have an impact on service delivery;
- believe that diversity within cultures is as important as diversity between cultures;
- respect the unique, culturally defined needs of various client populations;
- recognise that concepts such as 'family' and 'community' are different for various cultures and even for subgroups within cultures;
- understand that people from different racial and ethnic groups and other cultural subgroups are usually best served by those who are a part of or in tune with their culture;
- recognise that taking the best of both worlds enhances the capacity of all.

Suggested outcomes of cultural awareness training are for staff to:

- gain more of an understanding and appreciation of different cultures and practices;
- become more aware of their own culture, values, beliefs and behaviour;
- accept other people's culture, values, beliefs and behaviour in a non-judgemental way;

- develop an awareness of not making assumptions about cultural influences;
- appreciate that individuals' values and beliefs can vary within a culture;
- understand the different forms of communication appropriate for each culture.

Bus tour

Organise a bus tour around the local neighborhood for school staff so that they can see and experience the different cultures within the community. Set up guided tours of the local mosques, temples, synagogues, etc. and arrange for families to greet the staff at key points. This in itself helps to increase the cultural competency of staff which will help with the understanding and engagement of parents.

Tell us about you

Honour families and their culture by inviting them into school during staff meetings and/or training days to share information about their culture, community and religion. This will not only give staff a better insight but will also help to form good relationships.

Welcome

Reception staff

According to Samway and McKeon (2007), some families may feel uncomfortable in school settings where they feel pressured to speak English. Therefore, where possible, employ bilingual staff at the front desk so that they can greet and converse with parents. If this is not possible, engage bilingual volunteers who match the linguistic needs of parents to be at the front desk for one day a week and inform parents of this service so they can utilise it when needed. Another option is to provide a basic bilingual course for front-desk staff so that they can greet parents in their own language.

Signage

A school needs to make parents feel that it is a welcoming place where they can feel relaxed. One way to help achieve this is to display clear signage. As highlighted in Unit 2, signage is important for all parents coming into the school. It is equally important for the signage to be in different languages as well as Braille.

Guided tour

Every term organise a guided tour of the school for multicultural parents, providing basic information written in their spoken language and also hiring an interpreter for the session. This will provide parents with an insight into their child's school as well as providing the opportunity for them to ask questions.

Welcoming words

Organise a multicultural event where families explore the word 'welcome' in different languages and cultures. The words for 'welcome' can be displayed in the reception area of the school for all to see and feel welcomed.

Fly your flag

Invite parents into school to work with their child on creating a national flag of the world using a template so that all flags are the same size. During the activity ask families to research one interesting fact about that country to share with other families at the end of the session. All the flags can then be displayed in areas of the school where parents gather to help create an inclusive environment for all.

Did you know?

Ask families to research five facts about their culture/country, which can then be posted on the school website on a page titled 'Did You Know?' Parents can be directed to the page via the school newsletter.

Welcome packs

Welcome packs for parents are incredibly important as they can contain specific information regarding the school and their child's education. This is described in more detail in Unit 2. Having the welcome packs translated into different languages is a wise investment and will make all parents feel respected and valued.

Communication

Schools need to be able to communicate with multicultural parents, starting with clear and understandable English language. Clear communication must be considered for letters, signage, website, newsletters, etc. For other languages, involve interpreters and translators in order to connect with families and strengthen the home–school partnership. For more information on effective communication, see Unit 2.

Translators

The use of translators in multicultural settings is key in order to convey information as well as understand parents' needs and answer any questions and queries. There are different types of translators. Professional translators and staff, parent or student translators are all equally beneficial, although consideration needs to be given to the level of competency (spoken and written) and being involved in confidential meetings and discussions. When using a professional translator, ensure that they are fully versed in the school's education terminology and systems so that they can translate accordingly to ensure clear understanding. There are many professional translation services available such as Language Line (www.languageline. com/uk).

Parent meetings and consultations

During these types of meetings it is advisable that a professional translator is used or a member of staff fluent in the chosen language. Confidentiality is vital and it is also important to eliminate parental misunderstanding due to error of translation.

Written material

For all written material including leaflets, the school prospectus, letters, policies, newsletters, etc. employ the services of a professional translator. This ensures that the language is free from jargon and slang as well as being grammatically correct.

Meet and greet

For meeting and greeting parents both in school and the community, parent volunteers and students can be used.

Point of contact

There are countless benefits of having bilingual members of staff available within the school to facilitate communication to non-English speakers, for example:

- being able to support parents in helping their child with homework;
- providing information and reminders about key events;
- signposting parents;
- gaining parental opinions and feedback;
- being able to check for understanding;
- improving parent/school relationships;
- encouraging parents to engage with school;
- enabling parents to feel more involved as they have a designated member of staff.

Inform parents via the website or newsletters of the point of contact within the school who can support non-English speakers.

Parent partners

To provide another point of contact, recruit parents from minority groups to help engage and support other parents within the community and parents who may be new to the school. These parent partners can also provide a buddy system to help support parents in a number of different ways such as attending a meeting or overcoming language barriers.

Information badges

Ask bilingual members of staff to wear badges with the words 'How can I help you?' translated into the desired language. This works particularly well during key meetings, activities and/or events within the school and community.

Read all about it!

In order to reach as many parents as possible, place information in places such as supermarkets, corner shops, GP surgeries, job centres, public houses and leisure centres.

Communication styles

Work with all staff to develop their skills in communicating with parents using visual, auditory and kinaesthetic methods. This will help parents understand school information and also feel listened to and understood. Remember to be patient and speak slowly, especially when English is the second language.

Jargon-free

Put in a system so that all written information for parents is jargon-free. In order to meet parents' needs, explore delivery methods – for example, audio, visual, Braille, large print, dyslexia-friendly.

Printed material

It is a wise investment to involve parents right from the start in reviewing all the school's printed material (relevant to parents) for readability, including the school website, leaflets, prospectus, newsletters, etc. Parents can explore other channels through which to provide information and ensure the school's information meets parents' needs. Consideration needs to be given to parents who are visually impaired, dyslexic or have learning difficulties. The government has produced guidelines on 'Easy Read', a useful way of making information easier to understand through simple words and pictures (see www.easyreadsystem.com).

Different media

In order to increase accessibility, resources can be made available in a range of different media such as podcasts, video demonstrations, digital media, audio.

Newsletter

Translating regular newsletters and other information for parents can be costly so recruiting volunteers within the school and community can prove advantageous. Alternatively, when the newsletter is sent to parents, the family engagement officer (FEO) during home visits or school staff at the school gates can explain the key points to parents. Newsletters can also be translated and recorded, and then sent to parents as a podcast.

Website

In many cases parents who seek information will visit the school website, so having a translation button so that the site content can be translated into a range of languages is key. The product Recite enables visitors to customise the website so that it translates into up to 90 languages. In addition to working on the website, it can also be used on other devices. Consider translating all online forms and documentation.

Home visits

Having bilingual home-school liaison workers and assigning a family to one who speaks their language will go a long way towards engaging families. Set up a partnership with an English-language centre and ask them to join the FEO on home visits to non-English-speaking parents. This could be extended to providing a translation service for parents attending meetings, for example.

Events

Planning events

Involving parents from the start when planning multicultural events is a wise investment as it enables the school not only to tailor-make interventions and address the needs of the community but also respect family values and beliefs and benefit students.

Family technology night

There are many applications and platforms that are designed to communicate in a variety of languages. Once the school has decided on which one(s) to use, families need to be informed. Holding a family technology night is a great way to inform and support families in using the new technology in order to access school information. Below are some examples of such translation tools:

- voki.com
- imtranslator.com
- Google Translate.

Cultural fashion show

Host a cultural celebration fashion/clothes show involving students and families. The show can include different ethnic attires including faith-based dress, cultural dances and music providing the audience with an insight into the different cultures. The event can be followed by food made by the different families to celebrate a wonderful event.

Parents got talent

Ask families to enter the event Parents Got Talent (similar to the TV programme *Britain's Got Talent*) so that families can demonstrate their skills and talents – for example, how to cook a certain dish, perform a traditional dance, etc. The panel of judges can be made up of staff and parents who make positive comments rather than judging in the traditional sense.

Games from around the world

In every country around the world games are played, so having a 'games from around the world' themed evening enables families to have fun, develop their knowledge of other countries and also enjoy an element of competition. Select a number of fun games (ideas can be found at https://uk.pinterest.com/nsmtraining/engaging-families) and display the games around the school to generate interest among the students. Invite families to attend and present them on arrival with a map of the world which includes fun facts about the games. They can use the map to locate the games in the hall and take part either among themselves or with another family. Everyone records their score on a score card which can be handed in at the end of the evening to establish the overall winner.

Culture of the month

Highlight a different culture each week or month. Identify families that can assist with learning units in class and encourage them to do so. Create cross-curricular projects that have culture and ethnicity as a focus. Create posters saying:

- The culture of the month is . . .
- Did you know this . . .
- This week's interesting fact is . . .

To see an example of this go to https://uk.pinterest.com/nsmtraining/engaging-families.

Plan of celebration

Develop a plan that promotes the celebration of different cultures throughout the school year. Choose 12 cultures and each month celebrate by organising events/activities and for education during assemblies, newsletters, etc.

Parent views

Collect parents' views by conducting face-to-face or telephone interviews. This is an effective approach as it removes the barrier if a parent lacks literacy skills. It is also a great chance to ask parents which new opportunities/activities they would like the school to deliver.

Multicultural family night

Organise an evening to celebrate and learn about different cultures through information, food, song, dance, etc. Provide each family with a passport so that when they visit an activity, the staff member stamps their passport to validate their participation. At the end of the evening prizes can be given out to the families who have participated in all of the activities.

Multicultural column

In the school newsletter dedicate a column to multicultural information, events, activities, celebrations, etc. Make sure the column becomes an integral part of the newsletter so that parents look forward to reading it.

Multicultural library

Ask parents to help build a multicultural section within the school library by filling it with donated books, resources and information. Seek out funding for such a worthwhile venture.

To launch the library ask families to design a bookmark to honour a particular country and/or culture. Also include dual language books, dictionaries, etc.

Come dine with me

Just like the popular TV programme *Come Dine with Me*, invite families to bring a traditional plate of food into school to share with others. Food is always a great incentive to draw families into school and this way they have the opportunity to sample food from a different culture. Photographs can be taken of each plate of food with the recipe of how to make it which can then be either displayed on a designated board or printed in a book and handed out to parents so they can try making the dish at home.

International booth

At every major school event (e.g. sports day) have an international booth displaying multicultural information relevant to parents. The information can include signposting to services within the local community, key translated school information (e.g. forms, contact details, policies, etc.) as well as information on how parents can work with the school as volunteers.

Learning

Multilingual book club

Setting up a multilingual reading club within the school where parents can meet on a regular basis can really help support their children's education and encourage parents to read in their native language. Provide books in different languages and encourage students and parents to read to the group and/or to each other. Parents can take home story sacks containing activities, books and audio CDs to listen and read with their child at home.

Learn English online

There are many programmes online which can help parents and children learn English from the comfort of their own home. To introduce parents to these platforms, invite them into school for an information evening, provide refreshments and laptops, and take them through the different programmes according to their needs. Below are a few examples:

- Little Bridge – www.littlebridge.com
- British Council Learn English for adults – learnenglish.britishcouncil.org
- British Council Learn English for teenagers – www.britishcouncil.org/english/kids-teens
- British Council Learn English for children – learnenglishkids.britishcouncil.org

Homework

If a parent does not speak English, supporting their child with homework becomes a challenge. Where possible, provide multicultural books, textbooks and resources as well as the following:

- Translate homework and resources into the parent's first language.
- Provide 'Homework Help' workshops to show parents how they can help their child at home (e.g. practising reading by using wordless books).
- Find a tutor either from an agency or a member of the family to help their child's learning.
- Engage in a learn English online course.
- Watch educational television programmes and discuss them with their child.

Workshops for parents

Offer a variety of workshops for parents to help develop their skills so that they feel more empowered and also are more able to help support their child's learning at home. The workshops can be run in the community and/or school, offering training on:

- language classes;
- improving literacy/numeracy skills;
- ICT skills;
- teaching assistant qualification;
- learn to be a translator;
- rights and responsibilities;
- vocational qualifications;
- culturally sensitive programmes;
- British values.

Community

All ideas welcome

In order to reach as many parents as possible, speak to business owners and local places of worship and ask them for ideas on the best way to reach out to the families who engage with their service. Ask if school information can be displayed on notice boards or in shop windows to inform parents of key events.

Volunteering

Multicultural families tend to enjoy volunteering for culturally specific activities so involving them at the outset in the planning and organisation will generate more interest and engagement. Ask parents how they would like to volunteer in the school and/or community and what skills they can offer. It is important that all volunteers feel welcome and part of the school team so acknowledge, reward and celebrate their efforts and achievements.

Working with faith groups

Identifying and working with the key leader(s) within community faith groups is an effective and efficient way of reaching families. Faith group leaders can not only inform families of key meetings, events and/or activities within school but they can also attend themselves to provide reassurance for their families. They can also advise on organising and coordinating the best times for events to take place so that they don't collide with important festivals and times of worship.

Community school

To encourage more parents into the school building, open it up to the community and external organisations to run different clubs and activities. In this way families will become more familiar with the school layout and will be more likely to attend school-led events. It also provides a great opportunity to build partnerships with other organisations. Providing a one-stop shop at the school where families go to access a wide range of provision, courses, etc. will also help boost engagement not only because of convenience and familiarity but also because of the access to translation services.

Unit 7: Difficult-to-engage parents

Difficult-to-engage parents

Engaging with difficult-to-engage parents – also sometimes referred to as hard-to-reach parents – can be challenging for many schools. Unfortunately, for some families engaging with school may not be as straightforward as it may seem for others, due to a number of influencing factors. The term 'difficult to engage' is used to describe parents who may be difficult to reach or involve in school and their child's education. Desforges and Abouchaar (2003) identified the following factors as influencing home–school relationships: social class, maternal level of education, material deprivation, maternal psychosocial health, single-parent status and, to a lesser degree, family ethnicity. It is important that schools are persistent when wanting to involve hard-to-reach parents (Aronson 1996), and that they understand these barriers and are able 'to see the world through the eyes of parents who do not fit the norm' (Crozier and Davies 2005) in order to create effective partnerships to aid their children's education.

There are many misconceptions in the minds of the general public and of teachers about why some families are regarded as being 'difficult to engage'. Consider these statements:

- Her mother was hopeless at school, so what can you expect?
- If parents don't attend school events, it shows they don't care about their child's education.
- Parents who are illiterate and/or unemployed can't help their child.
- Children from working-class backgrounds and certain estates are all troublemakers.
- Considering how Amy performed in school, is it any wonder that her sister's academic performance is so dreadful?
- Families who are non-English-speaking in the home don't understand how to help and support their child's learning.
- It is acceptable only to contact families when a child has misbehaved.

These kinds of statements typify the low expectations that some teachers and members of the general public may have about certain families when challenging situations occur. These views tend to be held by professionals who always blame students or their parents' short-comings on the home rather than questioning their own or their school's actions. Research since that of Rutter *et al.* (1979) has consistently shown that what happens inside individual schools and classrooms really matters and makes a significant difference to the performance of students. At the same time, Dalziel and Henthorne (2005) did find that certain families, such as those containing a persistent school absentee, held more negative views towards teachers and their schools and made fewer voluntary visits to schools to foster and promote good home–school relationships.

Find out what barriers are preventing engagement. Often schools believe that it is because parents are not interested, but there may many other factors, such as:

- physical illness;
- mental illness;
- family breakdown;
- domestic violence;
- substance abuse;
- working parents who have limited time;
- parent's own negative experience of school;
- distrust of other parents and staff;
- communication/learning difficulties;
- low self-esteem and self-confidence;
- no recognition of the value of education;
- full-time carer of family member;
- English is the second language;
- lack of transport;
- no childcare provision;
- a lack of understanding about what is wanted from the interaction.

> The parent who will not engage is often the most difficult barrier to overcome. School staff work hard to foster positive parental involvement . . . They may, however, also need to challenge a parent's conduct or behaviour if it is putting their child at risk. This fine balance is made even more difficult if they can no longer have a dialogue with the parent.
>
> (Rogers 2009)

Hard-to-reach schools

The term 'hard to reach' is often used to describe parents who don't access school and don't respond to communications from school. This rather loaded phrase puts the emphasis on the inaccessibility of parents, but in reality it is the schools that are hard to reach for some parents. So consideration must be given to establish which (if any) part of the school is hard to reach. This can be established via surveys, asking parents and forming a parent forum to establish areas that are not working for parents and inviting suggestions about how to make the school easy to reach. Schools also need to consider why they label some parents as hard to reach. If this is because the parent doesn't come into school, then consideration must be given to why this expectation is in place and why school is not going to the parent.

Planning

Involving difficult-to-engage families in schools requires greater planning and understanding in order to achieve the desired results. Starting from where the parent is rather than where school would like them to be provides a solid foundation for engagement to take place.

Start early

Identify targeted parents early by gathering information from early years settings, primary schools or through multi-agencies who may have worked with the family. Early intervention or access to key information goes a long way towards understanding why a parent is difficult to engage and how school communication and engagement can be tailored to meet their needs.

Family engagement officer

Identifying a key worker, the family engagement officer (FEO) (see p. 34), to work with parents is important for a number of reasons:

- It provides a clear contact for the parents.
- Parents don't have to repeat the same information to different school staff.
- It provides an opportunity to build respectful and trusting relationships.
- The FEO can tailor-make support to meet a parent's needs.

> As a family support worker at Bensham Manor School I have improved parental engagement by simply having a work mobile phone. Parents prefer to contact me via my mobile phone rather than speak to the school office – for example, to discuss attendance issues. One parent who was always very hard to contact now prefers to send very long text messages rather than speaking over the phone. A few weeks ago I started using WhatsApp which means as long as the parents have internet access they can contact me without having to incur charges. I find it's the simple things which drive engagement.
>
> Alison Connor, Family Support Worker, Bensham Manor School

Parent ambassadors

Training parents to become ambassadors can help reduce suspicion or mistrust around school as well as improve attendance at meetings, events and activities organised by the school. Parent ambassadors can also:

- work alongside the FEO and link with local agencies to help signpost parents to the support they need;
- monitor the effectiveness of home–school communication;
- raise awareness of school meetings, events and activities.

> One important strategy in tackling [the issue of disengaged parents] has been to draw on resources already deeply embedded in the community ... support workers who live within and know the community well and can gain the trust of parents who feel challenged by direct engagement with schools.
>
> National College of School Leadership, Leadership for Parental Engagement

Start where each parent is at!

A one-size-fits-all approach for parental engagement is not productive when working with parents who are difficult to engage. In order to engage this parent category, schools must plan to start where each parent is at rather than where the school wants/needs them to be. Approaches and expectations must therefore be flexible so that they fit in with the parent rather than expecting the parent to fit in with the school's approaches and expectations. An article from Futurelab at the National Foundation for Education Research, 'Keeping it in the family', comments that some schools treat parental engagement as an expectation of families, but that schools instead need to consider the parent's needs and then formulate a plan to work with them.

> Not all parents are angels. All are individuals – accept the real person in front of you. Be prepared to work where each one is. The way they were treated in the past, and the way the present is bearing down on them makes some parents appear negative. Get past that wall with your acceptance and sincerity.
>
> (Peterson 1982, in Edwards 2006)

What's in it for me?

Make sure engagement is purposeful and promote the 'What's in it for me?' factor. Some parents may be focused more on 'me, myself and I' – 'What's in it for me?' and 'Will this benefit me?' When publishing a meeting, event and/or activity, ensure that you address 'What's in it for me?' and that the benefits of attending are clearly listed. For example, by attending you will get:

- a bacon roll and a cup of tea/coffee;
- a free crÉche facility for your younger child;
- to have time with your child's teacher to discuss their progress;
- a chance to purchase your child's framed piece of art work;
- to see your child perform on stage;
- a chance to win a hamper worth £ . . .

Disguising meetings, events and activities can also prove advantageous. For example, rather than inviting a parent to an online safety information evening, instead invite them to a bingo night and in between each game cover the relevant information from the online safety evening. Asking open questions can help to reveal the 'What's in it for me?' factor as parents are more likely to open up and reveal their interests and desires. Closed questions might start with 'Did you . . .?' and usually have a 'yes' or 'no' answer. Open questions usually start with 'What . . .?' 'When . . .?' and 'How . . .?' and require a more detailed response. For example:

- What would you like/need in order for you to attend this activity?
- How comfortable are you coming into school?
- How could I modify this meeting to meet more of your needs?
- How are you feeling about all of this?

Parent engagement funnel

The acronym AIDA (Attention, Interest, Desire and Action) provides an effective parent engagement funnel. This model helps to ensure that the steps a school takes in engaging parents are as effective as possible. It is designed to grab the attention of the target audience and engage their interest. Then it creates a desire within the parent to want to engage, whether for a meeting, event and/or activity being organised by school. Below the AIDA model is discussed in more detail.

Step 1: Attention

The first step is to capture the parent's attention. To attract their attention, consider the question 'What's in it for me?' (see p. 86).

(see p. 86)

Step 2: Interest

Once you've got the parent's attention, you need to keep their interest and this can be achieved by understanding and addressing any concerns or needs they may have before they consider taking action. Parents may be asking the following questions:

- Does this school/member of staff care about me?
- Does this school/member of staff understand me?
- Do I trust this school/member of staff?

Step 3: Desire

The interest and desire parts of the AIDA model go hand in hand: as the parent's interest is being generated, consideration needs to be given to needs and wants. For example, rather than offering the parent a workshop on 'Praising your child', address what's in it for them and rephrase: 'Boost your child's motivation, self-esteem and resilience. Learn the secrets of effective praise.'

Step 4: Action

The final step is the parent's engagement in the meeting, event and/or activity.

Venues and times

Venues and times of meetings, events and activities can provide an immediate barrier for some parents. Below are questions to consider when looking to involve those who are difficult to engage:

- Where do families tend to gather within the community and when?
- Where do local dads, ethnic minority groups, working parents, etc. tend to gather? Can information about school events be published in these locations?

- Where do most parents work? Can school access time with the parents through the employer?
- Do parents use local childcare facilities? Can information about school events be published at these services?
- Can the event be held at a venue in the local community where parents are more likely to engage?
- Can the event be held at different times throughout the day?
- Are there easy transport links to and from the event? Can transport be offered?
- Do parents need an interpreter?

Outside school visits

In some cases, before parents come into school, school must go to them, whether at their home or a place that is less threatening to parents. Where possible, always start a meeting with something positive about the child and spend time to establish the needs of the family and gain a better understanding, rather than talk about behaviour, attendance or standards (unless the visit is for this purpose). In order to make an impact, it is necessary to invest time in trying to understand the issues of uncertainty the parent may have and consider ways to acknowledge and thank parents for their contribution and attendance.

Home visits

- Through the parent involvement policy (see p. 21) inform all parents that home visits are commonplace; this ensures that no parent or student feels singled out.
- Formulate a plan and establish target families requiring home visits.
- Set aside strategic times during the year for home visits.
- Ensure flexibility around dates and times for home visits.

Community locations

- Identify rooms and locations within the community for important school meetings.
- Set a goal to hold a percentage of meetings, events and activities within the community.
- Choose locations according to the type of parent you want to engage (e.g. the local football club for dads).
- Set up a workshop/meeting at a local business where a group of parents work.

Pop-up school

A pop-up is the latest trend for bars and restaurants to open for short periods of time in key locations to test the market and promote their brand. Schools can also capitalise on this effective marketing approach. A pop-up school can be set up in key locations, such as a local supermarket at a certain time during the day or during a particular week so that parents can access information and talk to members of the school staff while remaining in their comfort zone. This approach of going to where parents are rather than waiting for parents to engage with school is a way of connecting, breaking down barriers and developing relationships. The pop-up can also take the form of a family engagement bus which can go to different locations within the community and provide the same support.

Transport

A lack of transport can be one of the many barriers some parents face when asked to attend school, if the parent:

- does not have access to a vehicle;
- lives remotely from the school with limited transport links;
- has one vehicle in the family and conflicting work schedules.

Although lack of transport can be a potential barrier, there are many practical solutions:

- walking bus;
- contact a local taxi company to work with the school in supporting parents living remotely;
- provide bus and/or train passes for key events;
- promote a car-share system;
- create transport vouchers that can be acquired via a school loyalty card system.

Calendar

It is important to note that not all parents may have or use a calendar and this may one of the reasons they don't engage with school. Providing a calendar at the beginning of the year listing all planned meetings, events and activities, and putting a call to action on key dates listed in newsletters so that they are added to the calendar, can prove very effective. A calendar enables parents to:

- keep track of school meetings, events and activities;
- remember other appointments (e.g. dentist, GP);
- plan effectively and meet deadlines;
- ensure their child takes the correct equipment into school on certain days;
- plan daily, weekly and monthly activities;
- remember important dates.

Fridge magnets

Fridge magnets are a great and inexpensive way to remind parents of key events as most families have fridges at home where they can be displayed. The magnets can be distributed to parents during parents' evenings or whole-school performances at the end of term. Consider printing the magnets in different languages. The magnets can display the following information:

- school mission;
- contact information;

- contact information of dedicated member of staff (i.e. family engagement officer);
- dates of key events.

Virtual tour of school

One of the many reasons parents don't engage with school is that they have had a negative experience of school themselves in the past and in some cases when attending their child's school. Negative experiences based on their own school experience will still form a barrier to engagement even when the school's decor, values and ethos are completely different from what they experienced. In these cases, providing a virtual guided tour, uploading it on to the school website or secure platform and sending an invitation link to parents can be the first step in breaking down the barrier. Involve staff and students in creating the film, taking the viewer into all key rooms and introducing the members of staff with whom the parents are likely to have contact. The virtual tour can have many benefits:

- It provides access 24/7 for the parent to walk through the school as if they're actually there.
- It allows parents to 'meet' the staff within the comfort of their own home.
- It can show parents exactly what the school looks like and has to offer.
- It provides more information and reassurance than a photo.
- It is a useful tool for staff members to show parents during a home visit.
- It can be played in the foyer area of the school.
- It is a strong tool for aiding a parent's decision to engage.

The grown-up method

There may be some parents who are so overwhelmed with personal problems that they don't have the energy left for their child's education. Identifying another person in the child's life is key in such a situation. The grown-up method is a great way to get children to think outside the box and engage more family members as a result. First, define what a grown-up is to the class, then ask each student to make a list of all the grown-ups in their family – for example, mum, dad, stepdad, aunty, gran, older brother. Once the list has been compiled, the child's main caregiver must confirm that they give permission for their child to work with the adults listed. Once approved, ask the class: Who on your list of grown-ups:

- can help you with your homework this week?
- is available to attend the parent meeting on Wednesday?
- can take part in the evening of fun activities on Thursday?

Once the student has identified the grown-up, ask them to write a personal invitation to attend (see below). If a chosen grown-up is not the parent and the parent is categorised as difficult to engage, then this provides a wonderful opportunity to develop a trusting relationship with the family member and create a 'back-door' form of communication into the home.

Over time this can help to break down barriers and provide the parent with the confidence to buddy-up with that family member and engage with school.

Personal invitation

One of the most powerful incentives for parents to attend school is for their child to send a personal invitation. This can be in the form of a letter, postcard or invitation card. Ensure the invitations contain all the required information as well as key benefits for attending. Using the grown-up method, the student can identify which member of their family will be available to attend the meeting, event or activity on the date and time given. The student can then send them a personal invitation which in itself addresses the 'What's in it for me?' factor. Leading up to the date, a personal invitation from the teacher also goes a long way to make the chosen grown-up feel welcome and may help to remove potential barriers to engagement.

Disguise meetings and events

Instead of advertising a meeting or event to parents with titles such as 'Parents' evening', 'Online safety talk' or 'Improving your child's literacy', use a disguise to address the 'What's in it for me?' question (see p. 86). By addressing this question, it will be likely that more parents will attend. So, for example:

- Instead of 'Parents' evening', advertise a 'Decorate a box' evening. While parents are waiting for their turn to talk with the teacher, they can take part in the creative activity with their child.
- Instead of 'Online safety talk', advertise a 'Bingo night'. Between each game of bingo give a 1–2-minute input about online safety.
- Instead of 'Improving your child's literacy', advertise a 'Curry night' and share key skills regarding literacy while families are enjoying their meal.

Of course, it is important that the information sent to parents does inform them of the true nature of the event.

Make it fun

Fun and enjoyment make things more inviting and contagious, so working to ensure that school meetings, events and activities are memorable is a wise investment. Most parents are more likely to engage if they feel part of a group that's having fun while achieving a goal. Keep sessions warm, welcoming, upbeat and positive, celebrate successes however small, and provide refreshments. Remember:

- make it valuable;
- make it shareable;
- make it memorable;
- make it fun.

Comfort zone activities

These types of activities can include anything that engages a particular parent/community. Providing a crÉche and food will also encourage attendance. Below are some examples of activities:

- fitness classes;
- relaxation and stress management;
- ICT;
- salsa dancing;
- cooking;
- dressmaking or embroidery.

Buddy-up system

Parents who want to engage with school but feel nervous or lacking in confidence can be buddied up with another parent or a friend. A buddy-up system can:

- provide support and a friendly face to a new parent;
- remind parents of key meetings, events and activities;
- provide support during a meeting with a teacher;
- help improve student attendance and reduce lateness;
- encourage voluntary work within the school;
- provide friendship;
- encourage other parents to get involved by bringing them along to an event.

School loyalty card system

Just like loyalty cards in shops and coffee houses, the school loyalty card system works by rewarding parents for engaging with the school. Parents can be given a designed card (size of a credit card) with shaded areas to be stamped (for an example, see www.nsmtc.co.uk/resources). Parents are given an incentive for getting the required number of stamps – for example, get six stamps and receive a free ticket to the end-of-year school trip. Each area requiring a stamp asks the parent to engage in a meeting, event or activity. For example:

- volunteer at the school fete;
- attend their child's class assembly;
- support their child with a home activity;
- attend parents' evening;
- complete and return a school survey;
- attend a literacy skills workshop;
- join the school/community choir;
- read at home with their child.

To ensure each has been completed, evidence is required in the form of a photo or attendance, and then the stamp is issued. For parents who actively engage with school, introduce a tiered system where they can also achieve gold, silver or bronze status.

Word of mouth

Parents often engage with school based on recommendations from people they know – in other words, through word of mouth. This method is an effective and inexpensive way to engage parents. Create a card (the size of a business card) and include a 'call to action' to let parents know that you would love to hear about their experience. This could be a straightforward 'Thank you for attending. Do you know of another parent who would enjoy a similar activity in school? Can you invite them to the next one?' For more tips, see Unit 2.

Loaning system

For some disadvantaged parents, buying resources for their child may be problematic. In these cases, a school loaning system can work really well, providing parents with the opportunity to borrow books, art resources, games, CDs, etc.

School cafe

An in-school cafe provides an informal environment where parents, staff and students can get together over a cup of tea or coffee. A cafe in the reception area can provide an instant welcome and put parents at ease, and at a set time during the day parents can be invited for tea, toast and a chat. The school can also recruit parent volunteers to run the cafe.

Internet cafe

A great service to offer in school is an Internet cafe. A survey by the Office of National Statistics suggest that about 5 per cent of children – around 300,000 – still do not have Internet access at home. An Internet cafe can offer parents access to:

- the Internet;
- facilities in the day and evening;
- scanning and printing facilities;
- courses designed to get the most out of the Internet.

Family room

A family room provides a dedicated space for parents within school where they can meet, learn and access resources (e.g. the Internet). It is a good idea to get parents to design and create the room themselves so they have ownership and are more likely to use it. The family room can provide parents with access to information and training including:

- family bulletin board;
- termly calendar of meetings, events and activities;
- debt management training;
- parent support networks;
- back-to-work schemes;
- first-aid courses.

No-show parent

Plan for if/when a parent doesn't show for a meeting, event or activity. Below are a few examples:

- If appropriate, make a recording of what they missed and arrange a home visit to drop off the recording.
- Send a letter home: 'Dear Mrs Fletcher, I am sorry I missed you at Tuesday's parents' evening. If you'd like to arrange another time to meet either at school or somewhere within the community, then let me know. Kind regards, Mrs Morgan.'
- If a parent hasn't attended parents' evening and seen their child's work, then create a 'take home folder'. The folder can include samples of the child's work, positive comments from the teacher and a few home activities. Also include a simple feedback/comment form for the parent to complete:
    - Did you enjoy looking at your child's work?
    - Which was your favourite piece of work?
    - What did you like about this piece of work?

An example of involving the difficult-to-engage using Time Credits

Herbert Thompson Primary school in Ely, Cardiff, has been part of the Time Credits project since September 2014. The school has focused on family and student engagement, working hard to encourage hard-to-reach parents to participate more often in daily school life. By earning Time Credits, families have been able to spend them on a range of family activities with some of our amazing partners, and recently families visited London with their Time Credits that they had earned over the 2014/15 school year.
   The head teacher said:

> For many of the children the highlight of the day was seeing the Crown Jewels and some children were so enthused by their visit that they conducted their own research into historical topics when we returned. The most overwhelming gain was on the children's own self-esteem; they worked so hard within their own roles to earn and save up the Time Credits and felt they had really achieved something.

Year 6 students earned Time Credits throughout the 2014/15 school year through focused projects, including being reading buddies and maths buddies for younger students within the school, litter picks within the school grounds, being hall monitors and assisting with school events. Over the year the children banked all of their Time Credits (over 600 hours!) in order to pay for the trip to London. Parents have been earning for coming in to read with their children, raising money as part of the PTA and assisting with numerous school events.

With the school's PTA fundraising for the cost of transport, the Year 6s were able to use their Time Credits to pay for entrance to the Tower of London, a ride on the Thames Clipper Boat and a trip on the O2 Skyline cable car. For the large majority of these students it was their first ever visit to London and the feedback was unbelievable.

> One of the mums said of the trip to the Tower: 'Time Credits have made a huge impact on both mine and my children's life! To be able to use Time Credits to take them to the Tower of London was just amazing – they talked about the trip all summer – and my boy is now obsessed with ravens!

By earning Time Credits throughout the year, it meant that the costs of the trip were significantly reduced for the parents which had a huge impact on whether their children could attend. Feedback from the school, the children and their parents was overwhelmingly positive and the trip was a resounding success!

The experience for all involved was incredible and the excitement about visiting the Tower of London played a huge role in getting people to earn Time Credits and get involved in school life throughout a whole school year.

The deputy head of Herbert Thompson School said:

> For us it has meant parents who would never work with the school have been regularly attending various activities, earning Time Credits and positively contributing – to then be able to use some of those credits to support their children to go to 'LONDON!!!' has really left some of them with a real sense of pride.

The reactions of both the parents and the children were also overwhelmingly positive. One parent spoke of how she has 'made new friends by joining the PTA, I enjoy going into school now and love giving my time, I loved banking the credits for the London trip!'

When we spoke to the children who attended, 100 per cent voted the experience as 'Excellent' and comments ranged from 'Time Credits make me feel proud . . . I really love helping . . .' to 'I want to live in the Tower'.

One particular child, who was a big Sherlock Holmes fan, loved that he could 'spend Time Credits where Moriarty got arrested!' and I believe the trip is neatly summed up by one of the children who simply wrote:

> Really, Really, Really AWESOME!

Community

Working with and forming community partnerships has many benefits such as:

- strengthening the school's resources and support networks with key agencies and support groups;
- sharing skills and knowledge through adult education;
- involvement in voluntary work;

- promoting family engagement;
- making a positive contribution to the community.

Go out!

Make time as a staff before the start of a new term to get to know the community and talk to families, helping to bridge the gap between home and school. The more parents see staff in their community, the more they will become familiar with them and will want to chat and engage. This type of interaction can make families feel welcome and eliminate any anxiety regarding the start of the new term.

A working lunch

Forming partnership links with local businesses can prove very beneficial when looking at engaging working parents. Ask businesses to offer a working lunch to parents so that during their lunchtime break they can attend a workshop to help support their child's learning. Linking with a cluster of schools will help target more parents.

Working partnerships with agencies

Form partnerships with agencies that will in most cases have already developed a relationship of trust with parents – for example, the health visitor. They can talk with parents on your behalf and also arrange a dual home visit. This will not only be productive in gaining access into the family home but will also help to overcome any misperceptions, negative assumptions or stigma about the purpose of the visit. Agencies can also be invited into school to provide a holistic support approach, offering services for parents (e.g. healthy eating, autism awareness).

> Partnership and multi-agency arrangements are an essential component of a comprehensive strategy for parental engagement.
>
> (Goodall and Vorhaus 2011)

Below is an example of how Ysgol Gynradd Gymraeg Tirdeunaw worked with the community to reduce reoffending.

Working with the community to reduce reoffending

School background

Ysgol Gynradd Gymraeg Tirdeunaw is a designated Welsh medium primary school in a deprived area on the outskirts of Swansea, South Wales, UK. There are 460 students aged 3–11 years on the register. Ten per cent of the children have experienced the imprisonment of a close family member. The well-being of all students is pivotal within the school and as a result of the support provided the academic achievements of all students, including vulnerable students, is high.

Partnership with Invisible Walls Wales (IWW)

The school was asked to work with IWW as they had a father of three children from the school. This pioneering new pilot project is based in Parc Prison, Bridgend, South Wales, UK. The aims of the project were to:

- prevent reoffending;
- prevent intergenerational offending;
- build links with the community after release;
- work with the prisoner and the family for a year before release and for six months' after;
- make fathers aware of their responsibilities towards their children (as they are six times less likely to reoffend if they have links to children when in prison);
- make offenders see the effect their imprisonment has on their children.

The family

The family involved with IWW consisted of young parents who were in an on/off volatile relationship with domestic abuse issues. Drugs and alcohol played a prominent role in their lives and they lived in poverty. Both parents had attended programmes to resolve their issues but they had proved unsuccessful. They had three children ranging from three to five years old. Their school attendance was 75 per cent. As a result of non-attendance, they found it difficult to form friendships, their academic achievements were below par and they were struggling to understand and communicate in Welsh. The wider family support was very strained at the time.

The school's additional learning needs coordinator (ALNCO) had previous involvement with the family as they had been on the Child Protection Register and Children in Need. Also as a class teacher, she had seen the effect that dad's arrest and imprisonment had had on the well-being of the children. The mum expressed her worries about explaining dad's imprisonment to the children and her ability to cope with her emotions and provide for them. Mum's honesty had enabled the ALNCO and social worker to support her at this difficult time. The school was eager to partake in the IWW project but, with the family's past history in mind, concern was expressed about the monumental size of the task ahead. This was particularly true as dad was initially very reluctant to cooperate.

Role of the school

The role of the school was to offer support to the students involved with IWW. All the staff were informed of the extra help needed. This included sessions with the school counsellor in our well-being 'Rainbow Room'. Father's day cards and pictures were sent to dad as well as school reports. The school supported Invisible Walls workers when they came to work with the children. Regular feedback on both sides was provided to ensure that all involved knew about progress and any concerns raised.

Contact was maintained with the dad in child protection meetings. A request was made to Swansea local authority to allow the dad to access the meetings via telephone conferencing. This gave him an opportunity to play his part and equally take responsibility along with the mother. This was a first for the authority.

Parents' evening

A key part of IWW strategy was to involve the dad in his child's schooling even though his was in jail. As a result, five members of school staff attended a parents' evening at Parc Prison. This was the first parents' evening to be held at a British prison. The dad was thrilled to see his children's work and to hear them read and speak Welsh for the first time. As a result of the support from the school, a parenting team, IWW and social services, the students' attendance was 98 per cent. Mum and dad could see the positive impact of this on their progress. All involved felt very proud.

Invisible Walls Wales – the effect on the family

The support of IWW when prisoners are released is fundamentally important to the success of the project. By the time the dad was released, the relationship between him and the mother of his children was over. The mother had a new partner and the relationship was unsettled.

Increased steps were put in place by all to protect them as home life was becoming increasingly difficult. Within a few months the signs were increasingly positive from the dad's perspective. He'd moved into a new flat. Following court proceedings, the children were removed from mum's care and placed full-time with dad. This was a complete change in all of their lives. Again the support network of school, social worker, IWW and Barnardo's was crucial. As a result, the children's attendance improved to 99 per cent. The professionals involved had no doubt that without the support and guidance given by IWW and the secure and constant framework of safeguarding and care put in place these three children would not be living together as a family today. This is indeed a success story.

Benefits to the school

Promoting the aims of IWW was extremely important to the school as 10 per cent of all students had experienced the imprisonment of a close family member. Because of the school's work with IWW, they had had access to the jail and a peek at how life is for the students, fathers and families when they are all separated. They have used what they had learnt through their experience in Parc Prison to the benefit of teachers, parents and students. The school's success in effective engagement was highlighted by ESTYN (school inspection) in 2015:

> The staff identify pupils' well-being needs particularly well and the school has a very effective programme of support for vulnerable pupils and their families. This includes visiting parents outside school. This is certainly one of the school's obvious strengths.

Unit 8: Working with parents to improve student attainment

Teachers and pupils are two of the key components in learning and schooling. But there is a third party in the equation: pupils' parents and families. Parents are their children's first and most influential teachers, and research has shown that parental engagement is a powerful lever for raising achievement in schools. Therefore, engaging parents and the children's wider and extended family is a very powerful tool in helping to build children's success both in school and at home. Research shows that excellent home-school links have a significant and positive impact on a child's performance at school (Fan and Chen 2001). A report written for the DfES (Desforges and Abouchaar 2003) showed that learning at home was the biggest influence on the achievement of children aged 3 to 7.

> School-based family and parent support activities should have the improvement of children's learning as a clear and consistent goal.
>
> (Goodall and Vorhaus 2011)

It is encouraging to know that the majority of parents are interested in their child's education, and recent research of parents surveyed in England showed they wanted more involvement. In the past 35 years, the time British parents spend helping their children with homework or reading with them has increased fourfold (Gershuny 2000). It is parents' support of learning within the home environment that makes a significant difference to their child's achievement. The following have been listed with reference to 'learning in families':

- formal, non-formal and informal learning;
- adults and children learning together;
- adults helping children learn;
- adults learning from children;
- adults learning skills in order to help their children learn.

Key research findings from Professor John Bastiani (2003) were:

- Children of parents who take an active interest in their schooling and show high levels of interest progress 15 per cent more in maths and reading between 11 and 16 years than other children.
- Gains in pupil achievement that stem from parental involvement programmes and activities tend to be permanent. In schools with matched intakes, those that do best have, among other things, strong links with parents and families; the reverse is also true.

- Family influences have a much more powerful effect upon children's attitudes and achievements than either school or neighbourhood factors – even when these are added together.
- Much of the variation in the achievement of 14-year-olds in English, maths and science is due to home factors.

The more schools engage parents in their child's learning, the more the message is reinforced that 'parents matter'. This often results in a more consistent and effective relationship between school and home, and a mutual understanding and working together on the learning process. The Department for Education (DfE) in 2009 highlighted the following excellent ways (especially modern technologies) in which schools can help parents to improve children's learning:

- sharing curriculum plans;
- using homework for parent support;
- parent access to curriculum materials;
- involving parents in lessons.

> School success must look beyond the school door. During the last 15 years education has concentrated on course curriculum, instructional methods and teacher training. Academic achievement is shaped more by children's lives outside the school walls, particularly their parents and home life. When parents and families are involved in school life there is a higher likelihood of better performance and a more positive attitude to school life.
>
> (Bogenschneider and Johnson 2004)

Barriers to learning

Some parents may have barriers to learning and these may not always be apparent. Such barriers to learning which may restrict parents from taking part include:

- attitudes towards education;
- low educational attainment;
- cultural background;
- English as a second language;
- learning difficulties;
- sensory difficulties;
- low aspirations;
- lack of self-esteem;
- lack of confidence when speaking to practitioners;
- impaired vision;
- impaired hearing;
- dyslexia;
- inability to read and/or write;
- lack of confidence or interest;
- lack of time;

- childcare problems;
- transportation difficulties;
- work commitments;
- lack of information about opportunities to learn.

Communication

Communication is key when engaging parents to help the raising of standards. Sharing as many successes as possible will keep parents up to date and let them know their child is doing well and what academic skills, social skills or knowledge they have mastered. Try to contact parents at least once every half term to update them on their child's progress, thank them for their support in home learning and share any positive news. Also send home a weekly work folder containing completed homework assignments, in-class work and any tests or quizzes that their child has completed. This works particularly well with hard-to-reach families.

> In schools with active communication with parents, children made better academic progress in reading and mathematics and showed better self-regulation.
>
> (Sammons *et al.* 2007)

Parents' reading level

When communicating with parents through the written word, it is important to be mindful of their reading level. Using short sentences and keeping the number of words over two syllables to a minimum goes a long way. Check the reading level of your texts by carrying out a free SMOG test (shop.niace.org.uk/readability.html).

Class website

The class website can be used to communicate with parents and keep them up to date as well as providing them with information on how to support their child's learning. Upload homework assignments, add the class Google calendar and list study sites including support videos to help parents to support homework according to subject areas.

Feedback phone call

Scheduling in a set time at the end of the day, week or month for a positive feedback phone call to parents can be very productive. The ratio of three positive phone calls home to one negative is a helpful framework for schools in changing a parent's response from 'What has he done now?' to a response that is more welcoming of positive news.

Online resources

- Edublogs is a free, safe blogging platform for teachers, students and school communities which keeps parents up to date on their child's education (edublogs.org).
- Kidblog provides teachers with the tools to help students publish writing safely online so that parents can access it (https://kidblog.org).

Supporting learning

Prompts for reflective thinking

Involving learners and families in goal setting

Some schools have 'goal-setting' evenings rather than parents'/carers' evenings – using a 'Visible Learning' 10 approach based on the research findings of John Hattie (2009). Learners are supported to assess their own performance and bring their parents/carers to the goal-setting evening where, with the support of a teacher, they explain to their parents/carers what they can do and what they aim to achieve by the end of the academic year. Because the learners themselves are leading the evening, this can result in a high degree of engagement from parents/carers, while also encouraging learners to take responsibility for their own learning.

Providing what information and feedback that parents/carers want

Parents/carers may well come to parents'/carers' evenings wanting to get other information, e.g. wanting to know whether their child is behaving well, how their child is doing relative to other children, whether the teacher knows their child and that they can they trust the school to care for them, whether behavioural issues are dealt with fairly, why their child is in a lower stream, etc. – see also the What parents/carers want section in the Reaching all families resource (Theme 3: Resource 3) in this toolkit. They may also come with information that they want to convey to teachers, or have bigger issues that they want to address, such as bullying. You may want to consider conducting a parent/carer survey (see activity at the end of this resource) to gauge the type of information families are generally seeking to receive and convey at parents'/carers' evenings. You may also want to consider whether you provide enough other opportunities for families to raise issues that require more time and space for discussion than parents'/carers' evenings allow (see the logistics checklist on page 72).

Communicating the school ethos and expectations of behaviour

Do you or could you use the parents'/carers' evenings to convey messages to families about the school ethos, the value the school places upon engagement with families, or the expectations the school has around behaviour and attendance?

Difficult conversations

Teachers are likely sometimes to have to deal with pushy or aggressive parents/carers or to have difficult conversations with parents/carers at parents'/carers' evenings. Do you provide enough training for staff on how to handle these situations? (See also the Development needs analysis for delivering FaCE resource (Theme 2: Resource 1) in this toolkit.) Is there an appropriate process in place for staff to follow should a difficult situation arise during a parents'/carers' evening?

Welsh Assembly Government (2014: 70)

Dine and learn

Host a lunch with families either during school hours or after school and choose a topic linked to student learning. Families can discuss the topics at their tables and complete activities while they enjoy eating a lovely meal. This creates a very relaxed atmosphere and therefore encourages learning.

Curriculum evening

Invite parents into school to see their child's work and what they have been learning. This provides a great opportunity for parents to ask questions and for teachers to update parents on key skills which they can use to support their child at home.

School library

Ask parents to help with the running of the library as well as organising reading events.

Stay and play

In early years settings parents can be encouraged to stay and play with their child and gain a better understanding of what their child is learning as well as meeting the staff. These sessions can be themed according to the learning outcomes for that day. This provides parents with additional skills to help support their child at home.

Family learning contract

A family learning contract is a written agreement between teacher, pupil and parents. The family learning contract clarifies what families and schools can do to help students learn and develop, highlighting the following:

- What are you going to learn?
- How are you going to learn it?
- Target date for completion.
- How are you going to know that you learned it?
- How are you going to prove you learned it?

Examples can be found on https://uk.interest.com/nsmtraining/engaging-families.

Learning journals

A learning journal is a great way to engage parents in their child's learning. Its purpose is to enhance learning through writing and thinking about what is being learned. It also provides an excellent platform for reflection regarding what the family did, why they did what they did, what they now think and what they now know. These learning journals can take the form of a notebook, an online application or an audiovisual format. The online learning journals pro-vide an excellent format and allow parents to use them wherever they are, as well as allowing other family member to access them. Some suggested starting points for parents using a learning journal with their child are:

- What have you learned about?
- Did you have any flashes or thoughts regarding whatever they have been learning?
- What do you understand so far?
- What do you need to know more about and how can you find this information?

Family learning room

There are many benefits to creating a family learning room within the school. These include:

- providing a space for parents to enjoy learning with their child;
- giving parents ideas on what a learning environment looks like and how they can repli-cate it at home;
- providing a loan system so that parents can borrow books, equipment, etc.;
- holding classes and information sessions to support child learning and development.

Involving parents in lessons

The Department for Education's *How Schools Help Parents to Improve Children's Learning* (2009) stated the following as excellent approaches (especially in modern technologies):

- sharing curriculum plans;
- using homework for parental support;
- parent access to curriculum materials;
- involving parents in lessons.

Involving parents in lessons can be achieved by their physical presence and/or through a live feed (e.g. Skype). The lesson can take many forms. Below are some examples:

- an opportunity for parents to learn what their child is learning;
- providing parents with the skills to help support their child's learning at home;
- parents teaching the class an interesting or useful skill;
- students teaching their parents what they are learning;
- inviting parents as guest readers.

STAR evaluation

When families have completed a piece of work or an activity, they can choose to complete a STAR (stop, think and reflect) sheet to evaluate what they have achieved. By stopping, think-ing and reflecting, families get to learn something about themselves. The following are some example questions which families can complete by writing, inputting online or answering during a discussion process.

• What did you both learn about growth mindsets this week?
• Which was your favourite growth mindset word or phrase and why?
• Which growth mindset activity did you both least like and why?
• How has developing a growth mindset benefited you both?
• Have you noticed any changes since taking part in the activities?

The most powerful question above is the last one: 'Have you noticed any changes since taking part in the activities?' When families identify a change, that in itself will motivate them to stick with it, learn more and set goals.

Positively reinforcing your child

A mindset is a simple idea discovered by world-renowned Stanford University psychologist Professor Carol Dweck over decades of research on achievement and success. Dweck identified two mindsets: people can have a fixed mindset or a growth mindset.

In a *fixed mindset*, people believe their basic qualities, such as intelligence or talent, are fixed traits. They spend their time documenting their intelligence or talent instead of developing them, and believe that talent alone creates success, without effort, which is wrong.

In a *growth mindset*, people believe that their most basic abilities can be developed through dedication and hard work. This view creates a love of learning and a resilience that is essential for great accomplishment. Research shows that people with this view reach higher levels of success than people with fixed mindset beliefs.

Teaching a growth mindset creates motivation and productivity in the world of business, education and sports. It enhances relationships and increases achievement.

Simply stated, we develop our mindset based on the different types of praise we receive with regard to our efforts. Therefore skilling up parents in effective ways to positively reinforce and give praise is key.

Family learning

> Parents have to engage with student learning in the home for any significant and sustained learning to occur.
>
> (Harris *et al.* 2009)

As most of a child's learning takes place at home, it is vital to support and skill up parents so that they feel more confident in helping their child learn. Family learning activities can help parents to understand how their child is taught and can also improve their skills in literacy, numeracy, ICT, etc. Table 8.1 provides suggestions for how to achieve this.

Adult community learning

These programmes are an excellent way of engaging parents to help improve their skills and understanding in order to help support the learning of their child at home. In some

Table 8.1 Some of the most effective ways in which families can support children to learn

Foundation phase	Primary school age 7–11	Secondary school age
Conversations that encourage children's natural inquisitiveness and love of learning while also developing language and communication skills.	Showing interest in their school and school activities.	Communicating the value of education, modelling respectful relationships with teachers and helping their child to feel that they belong in the school.
Role play, to encourage purposeful talk.	Communicating the value of education and helping them to feel that they belong in the school.	Taking an interest in the topics they are following at school.
Reading stories, talking about the pictures.	Ensuring that they go to bed at a regular time, have breakfast and attend school.	Keeping them focused on learning and homework, while also supporting their autonomy.
Teaching songs and nursery rhymes.	Spending ten minutes a day reading with the child – any text, anywhere.	Ensuring that they go to bed at a regular time, have breakfast and attend school.
Pointing out and playing with letters and numbers.	Using opportunities in daily life to use numbers and talk about how big/much/ many.	Communicating aspirations and celebrating achievements, both of which can be very powerful motivators for children at this age.
Painting and drawing.		
Developing one-to-one correspondence, e.g. matching socks.	Outings to museums, the library and art galleries and extra-curricular activities.	Providing an environment at home in which they can study (with no distractions).
Visiting the library, museums and galleries.	Working with the school to support the child with any particular issues.	Encouraging children to read, and to talk about the book they are reading, what they have read in the newspaper or the film they have seen.
Outdoor trips to parks, woods, beaches.	Supporting social and emotional learning.	Involving children in household tasks, such as how to understand bills and plan trips or plan spending/saving.
Supporting social and emotional learning.		Outings to museums, arts and cultural venues.
Helping their child to be 'school ready'.		Extra-curricular activities, such as sports or creative and cultural activities, that help them to apply their knowledge and develop social and emotional skills.
		Working with the school to support the child to work through any particular issues.
		Supporting course selection and guiding children in plans for post-16 learning.

Source: Welsh Assembly Government (2014: 19).

cases, schools might provide adult community learning on their own premises. Courses and programmes can vary in subject and duration, and sometimes qualifications may be obtained. Identifying what parents want is key to the success of adult community learning programmes.

Family learning classes

Set up family learning classes in school and invite parents to participate. Ask parents what they'd like to learn – for example, how to knit, create an app, improve their literacy, develop their understanding about healthy eating. These classes not only give parents the opportunity to learn but also provide a chance to share ideas with other parents. These types of classes can also help improve and support parents in their next steps in learning

Family literacy programmes

Research has found that family literacy programmes can have a significant impact on children's literacy outcomes. Providing parents with specific information on how to help support their child as well as key skills in reading, writing, etc., has greater benefits than providing parents with more general information.

Parent top tips homework guide

Form a focus group of staff and parents and create a parent top tips guide with easy reference to the following:

- how to build good homework routines;
- set up a homework station within the home;
- checklist: equipment needed;
- how to check what homework your child has been set and when it needs to be handed in;
- how to praise your child effectively;
- how to access teacher support;
- ways to talk to your child to promote learning.

Skills guides

- Create step-by-step guides on each area of education that will not only help parents to understand what their child is being taught in school but will also help them support and encourage learning at home.
- Establish the type of content guides that are most beneficial for parents and families.
- Keep the information simple and straightforward, avoiding jargon at all times.
- Create the guides in different formats – paper, web-based, video, audio.
- Hold a workshop to inform parents how to use and get the most out of the guides.
- Translate the guides into different languages.

Step-by-step video guides

Add step-by-step video guides to the school website to help parents support their child's learning at home. These can be links to relevant websites or teachers can create their own for each subject area. Provide a facility to allow parents to leave feedback on their experience.

> Parents who were given interactive homework and were trained on how to support that homework, doubled the amount of time they spent on helping their children . . . and their children performed the best.
>
> (Battle-Bailey *et al.* 2004)

Parents 2 tutors

An effective way to skill up parents to help support their child at home is to train them as tutors. As we know, parents are their children's first and most influential teachers, so this is a great way to capitalise on that.

- Develop a 'train the tutor' programme which can be accessed once a week for one or two hours in school.
- Select key skills to teach parents – for example, pedagogy, methodology and understanding the difference between knowledge questions and application questions.
- Ensure the training sessions are free of jargon as well as touching on all teaching styles.
- Inform what is needed to set up a homework station at home.
- Ask for feedback at the end of each session to ensure the information provided is relevant and at the appropriate level.
- Celebrate the end of the programme with a graduation ceremony.
- Inform parents of other training they can enrol in, either at the school or as part of adult learning.

Effective conversations at home

A little book of questions

Create a book of questions parents can ask their child at home rather than the typical question 'How was school today?' Asking questions about what their child has done helps parents become more aware of their own process praise and therefore generates a growth mindset. Below are some examples of questions:

- What did you enjoy most about your performance?
- How do you feel about what you just did?
- What did you practise today at football?
- What did you learn today in gymnastics?
- How did you create that?
- How did you do that?
- How did you figure that out?
- How many ways did you try before it turned out the way you wanted?
- Are you pleased with it?
- What do you think will happen if . . .?
- What did you do that was difficult today?
- How did you overcome those difficulties?
- Did you make any mistakes today?
- What did you learn from your mistake?
- Will you tell me about . . .?
- Can you show me . . .?
- What can you teach me about what you learned today?
- Can you explain the difference . . .?
- How do you get . . .?

These questions help to create new dialogue about school and ultimately encourage positive interaction between parent and child. Creating a little book of questions provides the parent with new ways of talking to their child.

Learning board

Invite parents into school to create a mobile three-panel learning board which, when erected, provides an instant learning area at home. The board can display homework assignments, school calendar, homework schedule, etc. Provide parents with a list of equipment their child will need when completing homework tasks.

Family outings

Home learning can also include family outings to historic sites, churches, libraries, museums and parks. A visit works particularly well if it is linked to what the child is learning in school as it brings learning to life. Families can be sent a list of questions or discussion points to work on, as well as being encouraged to gather information in the form of photos, literature, etc.

Online resources

- School Explained is a social enterprise committed to supporting parents with their child's learning at home. Created by teachers, their parental engagement tool offers expert advice so parents can help their children with confidence and clarity. Parents post a question and a qualified teacher answers it. See schoolexplained.com.
- Oxford Owl is a free parent support website designed and developed by Oxford University Press to help parents with their children's learning at home. See www.oxfordprimary.co.uk.
- Words for Life is a campaign from the National Literacy Trust which gets parents involved with their children's communication and literacy development. See www.wordsforlife.org.uk.
- The Literacy Champions programme connects community volunteers with local families that would benefit from advice about supporting their children's early literacy development. See www.literacytrust.org.uk/literacy_champions.
- The Young Readers Programme is a project that motivates disadvantaged children and their families to read for pleasure. See www.literacytrust.org.uk/nyrp.

Reading

Encouraging parents to read with their child is by far the simplest form of engagement with the most powerful results. According to international research by the Organisation for Economic Cooperation and Development (OECD), parents can improve their children's academic performance by the equivalent of up to six months' schooling by reading together, singing songs and even sharing family meals. Below are some more benefits of reading:

- creates a bond between parent and child;
- helps to build a child's vocabulary and develop pronunciation;

- encourages the family to learn new things;
- improves communication skills;
- encourages the acquisition of knowledge;
- develops hand-eye coordination and motor skills;
- improves the ability and understanding to follow a story from beginning to end.

Book club

A school book club is a wonderful way to instil a love of reading with students and also parents. By reading and discussing books, parents start to form special time with their child while helping develop a love of reading and important language and literacy skills. Setting up a book club will require the following steps:

- Locate a quiet and comfortable room.
- Consider the best day and time to hold the club.
- Decide on the number of sessions and duration (e.g. one hour every two weeks for half a term).
- Invite students and their parents.
- Nominate an adult facilitator.
- Provide refreshments.
- Formulate club rules (e.g. no talking when someone else is talking).
- Decide on the book.
- Agree on the book club name, e.g.
    - Books and Bagels
    - Chatterbox Reading Club

Family reading time

Families need to be encouraged to dedicate some quality reading time during the week or at the weekends. Family reading strategies can be given to families to help them support their child with reading at home. Creating the correct environment is essential if reading is going to be enjoyed by all the family. Once a family reading session is planned, the following ideas can be just the thing for a comfortable, relaxing reading session:

- Get the whole family involved, including grandparents, younger brothers and sisters.
- Families can read together, in pairs or individually.
- Have a family DEAR (drop everything and read) time.
- Have a dictionary and simple thesaurus readily available for the reading time, and a picture dictionary for younger readers to check the meaning of tricky words.
- Make visiting your local library a regular family essential.
- Reading is any material that stimulates or interests the reader - it can be jokes, riddles, poetry, facts, fiction or even plays.

Family book club

A family book club is a great way to bring families together, improve literacy and have fun. In some cases it's a good idea to start the family book club in school so that parents can be shown what to do, have questions answered and have the support of the school which can also include a book loaning system. Sharing up-to-date research based on the impact family learning programmes has on reading provides a great incentive. There are four simple steps when setting up a club:

1. Select a book

Family members take it in turn to choose a book. Multiple copies can be obtained from the local community or school library. For family members who have difficulty reading, an audio version of the book can be downloaded. For younger children, the adult can read the story to the child.

2. Set a time and place

Encourage families to set the same day and time every week to come together and discuss the book. This will provide consistency and improve sustainability.

3. Create the reading environment

The reading environment needs to be considered – for example, a quiet room away from any distractions, drinks and snacks.

4. Start the book club

Family members agree on the format the book club takes – for example, the order in which everyone reads, discussion questions, activities related to the book. (These can be found on https://uk.pinterest.com/nsmtraining.) Watch the movie based on the book. Go to an author signing at a bookstore.

Audio books

Listening to audio books as a family develops listening skills, can help with understanding complex language and conveys how to tell a story to keep people's interest. When encouraging reading at home, consider audio books as some family member may prefer this option for any of the following reasons:

- English is a parent's second language.
- Working parents who commute to and from work can listen while they travel.
- A parent has a learning difficulty, low literacy levels or is dyslexic.

- A parent is blind or visually impaired.
- A parent has attention deficit disorder.

Sharing books on Twitter

Set up a class Twitter account and create a hashtag for students, parents and teachers to write short book reviews. This also provides a great platform for book recommendations, questions, etc.

Online resources

Storynory has hundreds of free audio stories. See www.storynory.com.

Mystery reader

Invite parents to sign up to be the school's mystery reader. They can surprise their child and benefit the whole class with a wonderful story.

Once a week a different parent comes into class and reads a story of their choice in a language of their choice. On arrival, the class can cover their eyes and count down from ten, then open their eyes to reveal the mystery reader. A captivated audience is created – especially the child whose parent is reading.

Reading morning

This intervention invites parents to come to class on a certain day at a certain time to read with their child. It not only allows parents to spend time with their child but gives the teacher the opportunity to teach the parents key reading skills which they can practise at home.

The takeaway approach

Plan a takeaway activity after every event in the school calendar attended by parents. The takeaway activity can involve equipping parents with follow-up activities to help extend the lesson at home, skills to help support their child's learning, top tips and resources.

Story sacks

A story sack is a large cloth bag containing reading materials for parents to use with their child at home. The resources can include the child's favourite book, a puppet and a CD of the story. These bags are loaned out to parents, although it is more effective if parents attend a workshop at the school guiding them through the process so that they get the most out of it with their child at home.

Storybooks

Get families to create their own story books, including pictures and words. These can then be read at home or brought into school and shared with other families. Workshops can be introduced to show families how to create their book online using a variety of publishing tools.

Homework

Homework has many positive effects on students' learning, including raising achievement across all courses, developing as lifelong independent learners, developing study and work routines, and building positive links between school and home. When setting homework, the best practices that link teacher, student and parent will have the best outcome. Consider the following to ensure there is a benefit:

- How will the students benefit?
- How will the parents benefit?
- How will the teacher benefit?

To improve the success rate of homework completion and learning outcome, consider the following:

- Parents have been given the appropriate skills to help support their child at home.
- The student has implemented the grown-up method (see p. 90).
- The student's home has a designated homework area with the necessary equipment.
- Parents establish a healthy homework routine with their child.
- Parents are provided with a list of homework expectations and a system of dealing with non-completed homework.
- Parents are provided with a feedback facility option to comment on assignments.
- Parents know what is expected of them in supporting their child with homework.
- Parents understand the importance of homework and why it is part of their child's learning.

Homework club

Setting up and inviting parents to the school homework club provides a great opportunity for parents to work with their child as well as learn new skills in order to support their child's learning. Below are a few suggestions on engaging parents in this:

- Buddy up parents with other parents whose children have been already attending homework club.
- Offer parents the opportunity to help coordinate or assist with the planning and running of the club.
- Assess the effectiveness of the club by asking for parent feedback.

Online homework applications

Scheduling students' homework online provides direct communication to parents in keeping them up to date with what their child is learning and informs them of the homework that needs to be completed. These systems also allow parents to communicate back to school and ask for support if needed.

Online resources

- Frog Education allows parents to view, like and comment on their child's work direct from their dashboard. See www.frogeducation.com/products.
- Show My Homework App allows teachers to quickly set simple homework tasks. See www.showmyhomework.co.uk.

Unit 9: Working with parents to improve student behaviour and attendance

The involvement of parents in their children's learning leads to greater problem-solving skills, more enjoyment of school, better attendance, fewer behavioural problems and a better and more natural development (Melhuish *et al.* 2001). A child's life is greatly influenced by their parents, siblings, grandparents and other family members, and when schools create strong home–school links, the results show consistently fewer problems related to student work and behaviour.

> One of the most powerful but neglected supports for children's learning and development is family involvement both in and out of school. Over 40 years of steadily accumulating evidence show that family involvement is one of the strongest predictors of children's school success, and that families play pivotal roles in their children's cognitive, social, and emotional development from birth through adolescence. (Weiss *et al.* 2009)

Parental support is a substantial factor in enabling students to cope with and adapt to the demands of behaving appropriately in school. When a student exhibits behavioural difficulties in school, parents are a key resource in helping teachers to secure change in a student's behaviour. Without actively involving a student's parents in significant discussions about a student's misbehaviour, a school may reduce its own chances of securing improved conduct.

Schools need to understand that parents have much more time and more opportunities to influence and shape their own children's behaviour. A school's influence is for 38 weeks out of 52 each year and, in most weeks, for up to five days. Parents, on the other hand, are actively involved every day for 52 weeks of each year. When teachers think parents are contributing to the students' problematic behaviour, it becomes critically important that they try to engage with them. In the final analysis, a home appointment or visit may even be necessary.

> Parents, carers and families are by far the most important influences in a child's life. Parents who take on a supportive role in their child's learning make a difference in improving achievement and behaviour.
>
> (Scottish Executive 2006)

School behaviour policy

Keeping parents up to date about the school's behaviour expectations is not only a legal requirement but also vitally important to ensure parents' understanding of what appropriate behaviour means. In 2016 the Department for Education outlined the requirements for schools in their guidance document *Behaviour and Discipline in Schools: Advice for*

Headteachers and School Staff. Here it states, among other key points, that 'the headteacher must publicise the school behaviour policy, in writing, to staff, parents and students at least once a year' and that 'The school's behaviour policy must be published on its website (School Information (England) Regulations 2008)'.

School and class rules, whole-school correctives and positive reinforcements are only effective and sustainable when school staff, students and parents have a comprehensive understanding of what is expected and how the system works.

Behaviour management review committee

Invite school staff, students, governors and parents to form a behaviour management review committee to assess current procedures and systems as well as develop programmes and processes. The committee could convene once every term with an action plan to address behavioural issues before the next meeting.

Key questions

When implementing the school behaviour policy and working with parents to improve their child's behaviour, consider the following questions.

Does the whole-school behaviour management approach:

- differentiate strategies and approaches to manage challenging behaviour?
- work with parents to support students' social, emotional and behavioural needs?
- assess possible connections between students' conduct problems and their literacy and cognitive development?
- build supportive and trusting relationships with students' families to encourage and facilitate their social and emotional development?

Home–school agreement

A home–school agreement is a document explaining the school's aims and responsibilities as well as the responsibilities of the parent and students. Such an agreement also promotes student–parent–school engagement to form good working relationships. It is a legal document which provides clear communication to the home regarding expectations.

Social and Emotional Aspects of Learning

The implementation of social/emotional learning in school to help reduce unwanted behaviour and improve well-being is an essential component of the school's behaviour policy. Many schools tend to use SEAL (Social and Emotional Aspects of Learning) to achieve this. The programme provides a whole-school approach to promoting social, emotional and behavioural skills for students. The materials provide a wide range of resources that can be used across the whole school for managing behaviour and emotional learning. These include such facets as working in partnership with parents, problem-solving, assertiveness and circle time. The resources are aimed at providing schools with an explicit, structured whole-curriculum framework along with practical ideas for teaching social, emotional and behavioural skills to all children.

Year group agreement

Create a year group agreement listing all academic, behavioural and attendance standards and expectations. All students sign and date the document and it is placed in a central position in the classroom. If a student fails to comply with the agreement, they are required to write a letter to their parent(s) informing them of how and why they broke the agreement as well as what they plan to do next time. This not only keeps the parent(s) up to date with their child's progress but also gives the student the opportunity to reflect. In order to help the student writing this letter, they can use the Gibbs Reflective Cycle which consists of the following questions:

- *Description*: What happened?
- *Feelings*: What were you thinking about?
- *Evaluation*: What was good and bad about the experience?
- *Analysis*: What sense can you make of the situation?
- *Conclusion*: What else could you have done?
- *Action Plan*: If it arose again, what would you do?

School attendance

Research shows that parent involvement has a positive impact on school attendance, especially when schools implement the following:

- Inform parents on a regular basis of the school's attendance and lateness policy and expectations.
- Update parents on a regular basis of school procedures for notifying the school of a student's absence.
- Provide a dedicated attendance phone line and a designated member of staff to contact.
- Inform parents of top tips and strategies designed to encourage regular school attendance.
- Implement an improving attendance action plan.
- Implement a positive reinforcement plan to acknowledge and reward students for improved and sustained attendance.
- Visit the parent at home to discuss ways to improve their child's attendance.
- Set up a buddy-up system with students and/or a walking bus.
- Positively reintegrate absentees and parents with a warm welcome and a clean slate.

The walking school bus

A walking school bus is supervised by the required number of adults to students and is designed to walk students from home to school and in some cases from school to home. This programme has many benefits including:

- improving student attendance;
- involving parents as volunteers;
- improving student fitness and well-being.

Bicycle train

A bicycle train is a variation on the walking school bus; instead of students walking to and from school, they cycle under the supervision of adults.

Positive reinforcement to improve attendance and lateness

Research has indicated that positive reinforcement rather than a punitive approach motivates students and improves attendance and lateness. Reward systems such as Class Dojo, Vevo Stars, credits, merits, raffle tickets, wristbands and loyalty cards work well. Once a positive reinforcement system has been implemented, inform and explain to all parents as well as students. Include in the positive reinforcement system how parents are acknowledged when their child's attendance improves and is sustained. A simple thank you always goes a long way. Name the reward system for maximum impact, for example:

- Early Bird Scheme
- 100% Attendance Club
- Great Turnout Club
- In It To Win It Group
- Top TEAM (Together Everyone Achieves More)
- A Team.

Breakfast club for families

When parents drop their child off at school, invite them into a breakfast club. Here they can have tea and toast as well as a chat to school staff as a way of forming relationships in a relaxed environment.

Improve parents' perception of education

Research by Dalziel and Henthorne (2005) shows that students whose parents value education tend to have excellent attendance rates compare with those who have an 'anti' school and teacher attitude. Compiling a marketing campaign explaining the value of education to parents is therefore key.

Information sharing with parents

It is always a good idea to build a history of positive contact with parents. When schools establish such a history, it is much more likely that the parents will listen to their concerns and accept them should any problems with behaviour arise. Research has indicated that teachers are more likely to make contact with a parent when their child has engaged in unwanted behaviour or if their academic standards have dropped. It is therefore crucial that parents are contacted to celebrate their child's successes as this way parents will be more inclined to engage by taking the phone call or attending a meeting and will also be more cooperative if there is a concern.

Early notification to parents is normally best for two reasons. First, it helps to prevent behaviour from worsening. Second, schools and parents will start to work together at the earliest possible opportunity. Schools should try to avoid parents asking, 'Why weren't we told about this before now?' Schools should advise parents:

- When there are difficulties. All parents need to know when their child is experiencing difficulties in school.
- The scope and extent of the problems or difficulties. Parents need to know the extent of any difficulties in school so that they can compare this with their child's behaviour at home. They can then make a judgement on the nature of their child's needs.
- The school's approach to responding to a student's behavioural difficulties. Parents need to be advised of how the school intends to react to the problem(s).
- Providing advice to parents on how they can help and support the school and their child in dealing with and resolving the behavioural difficulties.

Online portals

One of the most efficient forms of information sharing with parents about their child's education, behaviour and attendance are online applications such as Go 4 Schools, Behaviour Watch, IRIS Connect and SIMS inTouch. Applications such as these are more effective when time is taken to train parents how to use the system and provide ongoing support as well as gathering feedback regarding the accessibility of the service. Below are a few benefits of using online applications for parents and schools:

Parents can access:

- real-time information 24/7 about their child's education, behaviour and attendance;
- information on their child's timetable to help organise bringing in the correct equipment and homework;
- up-to-date information and support on set homework.

Schools can:

- centralise their own recording systems;
- log incidents online;
- send automatic alerts to staff and parents when incidents are logged (a follow-up phone call by the member of staff who logged the behaviour is recommended);
- access analysis of student behaviour/attendance to highlight areas of concern;
- access real-time information when meeting with parents.

System to resolve problems

Providing a clear and simple system for parents to help them resolve problems and/or concerns can help to nip things in the bud and eliminate confusion. Parents need to know who they need to speak to and where to go next if their problem isn't resolved.

Home-school book

Home-school books can work particularly well, but for parents who have a low literacy level another form of communication may need to be implemented. The book provides dual communication from school and home regarding the child's learning, behaviour and/or attendance. The book can be sent home on a daily basis and is a vital link for exchanging information, ideas, challenges and successes. Encourage parents to provide any information on their child's positive and/or negative experiences at home which could impact on their school day. Such information not only benefits the teacher but also encourages the parent to observe and comment on their child's behaviour and therefore take an interest in what they see.

Phone call/postcard home

When starting a conversation with parents, lead with good news where possible. Every child at some point during the school day will have engaged in something positive, however small, so it is the duty of the teacher to find this and share it, and then, if required, discuss the concern. It is based on the behaviour rule that what you focus on, you get/see more of, so making a conscious effort to see more of the positive and guiding parents to see this too will ultimately bring more of it.

'Wish you were here' postcards

If/when a student is absent from school, either the teacher or class can create and send a 'Wish you were here' postcard. The postcard can contain information on all the exciting activities happening in school that week in order to encourage the student to attend. Or the postcard can convey the support of the teacher and class for the student and wish them a speedy recovery if they are unwell.

Class Dojo

The Class Dojo application is a free tool providing a communication platform to encourage students in learning, behaviour and attendance as well as engaging parents. Parents can use the application to review their child's progress and also communicate with their child's teacher. See www.classdojo.com.

Mobile apps

The following mobile apps allow short pieces of text to be recorded and sent to the parent:

- Tellagami is a free mobile app that allows the teacher to create an avatar of themselves and record a message and/or text to a parent. When the parent plays the message, they find that the teacher's avatar has synced with their voice. This is an effective tool if the parent is unlikely to pick up the phone.
- PhotoCard is a free mobile app which allows the teacher to send an electronic postcard to a parent, celebrating their child's success or updating them on achievements.

Home positive behaviour hotspot

Focusing on a form of misbehaviour which needs to improve is a very powerful way of reversing the undesired behaviour. Involving parents practically is a good way of transforming their child's behaviour through this approach as the parent is only requested to focus on one thing. The simplicity of this approach ensures a greater take-up and visible results will inevitably be seen. During the behaviour management review committee, discussions can take place around the types of student behaviour for which change is needed. For example:

- improved manners in a particular respect;
- attendance and lateness;
- bringing the correct equipment into school.

When a comprehensive list of behavioural hotspots has been compiled and the action agreed upon, they can then be implemented one at a time over a week, a month or a term. Parents can be informed of the home positive behaviour hotspot via newsletter, phone call or text or face-to-face. Inform parents that when they notice their child displaying the hotspot, they are to reinforce with acknowledgement and a token (tokens can be redeemed in school for house points, Veo Stars, Class Dojo points, raffle tickets, vouchers, etc.). Below are some examples of home positive behaviour hotspots which are worded in order to focus on what is wanted:

- saying please and thank you;
- leaving the house on time;
- packing the school bag with correct equipment.

Role models

Invite positive role models from the community into school to work alongside students. There are many benefits to this process, especially if the role model is carefully linked to the needs and interest of the student – for example, if a child is passionate about football, a footballer role model will provide a great motivator. By means of the process of neuro-linguistic programming (NLP) students can achieve an outcome – for example, improved attendance – by studying how someone else goes about it. This process of studying can be done both consciously and subconsciously.

Nurture groups

Nurture groups are an in-school specialist form of provision from early years to secondary schools. Group sizes are around ten students who spend most of their time in the teacher-led group but remain part of their mainstream class. The focus tends to be around creating a supportive, nurturing environment to help with the students' development as well as the ability to form positive relationships with both school staff and peers. Nurture groups are based around the six principles of nurture:

- Learning is understood developmentally.
- The classroom offers a safe base.

- Nurture is important for the development of well-being.
- Language is a vital means of communication.
- All behaviour is communication.
- Transition is important in the lives of children and young people.

(The Nurture Group Network)

Parent meetings

There are three types of parent meetings:

- general parent meetings;
- parent meetings; to discuss a concern;
- student-led conference.

General parent meeting

A general parent meeting is an excellent way to get to know the student's parent(s) and to share information regarding the child's behaviour, attendance, standards, etc.

Parent meeting to discuss a concern

Meetings to address concerns can be formal or informal. A formal meeting will probably include staff such as the headteacher, special needs coordinator (SENCO) and educational psychologist. An informal meeting will probably include just the FEO.

If the issue is related to the child's behaviour, accurate documentation of the facts must be collated. This will include previous exploration into possible triggers for the behaviour and the involvement of others. Ensure privacy of certain information – for example, do not mention the names of other children to parents.

The approach taken in this meeting will in large part determine the outcome and the future involvement of the parent and child. They should not feel it is a personal attack on them and they should be certain that you have considered all sides of the situation. Both parent and child need to see that the FEO is helping rather than judging or criticising. The parent should be encouraged to suggest ways of moving forward and to implement ideas to help their child. Once a plan is agreed upon by all parties, establish a timeframe for its implementation and subsequent review and any next steps. In this way the situation can be closely monitored and any developments tracked.

Assessment form questions

To help achieve the desired outcome for this type of meeting, the Solihull Approach Assessment Form questions may be used as a guide (see Douglas 2004). This assessment aims to build an understanding of the situation, which will then often indicate the next step. Asking a series of questions and writing down the answers can sometimes hinder building the relationship, so the questions should be treated as a guide. They cover areas that contribute to the story you will be constructing with the parent and child about the nature of the problem and how it arose. The assessment questions for particular difficulties will indicate whether you need to make an immediate referral to a specialist service.

1. What is the parents'/young person's perception of the difficulty and expectations of the child/young person?
2. What is the parents'/young person's perception of normal behaviour?
3. What is the parents'/young person's previous and current management of difficulty (e.g. praise, punishment, coercion)?
4. What is the child's/young person's medical/social/emotional history?
    (a) Pregnancy, birth history, birth weight, early childhood. What was the pregnancy and birth like? How did the mother and baby bond?
    (b) Health issues: any current medication?
5. What is the developmental status (e.g. language skills, hearing, comprehension, concentration span)?
6. What recent life changes (e.g. new baby, family bereavement, change of carer) have there been?
7. What are the family routines (e.g. day care, meals, sleep)? Does the family have routines?
8. What are the main features of concern?
9. Are there any patterns to the child's/young person's difficulty? What triggers the difficulty?
10. What do they think started the difficulty?
11. Are the child's/young person's carers working consistently with the child/young person and do all carers agree about the problem?
12. Do the parents/young person understand the developmental norms of behaviour and the emotional development of the young person/child?
13. What does the mother/father think about the child/young person generally?
14. Do you think that the child/young person is using his/her behaviour to express distress or anger?
15. Do the parents have their own issues around management of the difficulty?
16. What are the parents'/child's/young person's view of family life?
17. What are the parents'/child's/young person's view of school life and friendships?
18. What are the parents'/young person's goals for improvement?

If the issue is learning related – for example, you are concerned that a child is underachieving – the meeting needs to be handled tactfully so as not to make the child feel stupid or make the parent feel blamed. However, if the parent is hearing for the first time that their child is underachieving, it is important to establish why that is. If this is the first they have heard about it, the parent's first instinct might be to blame the teacher, the FEO or the school.
    Preparation is key:

• Have evidence of the student's current achievement and how this relates to age-related expectations. Make the point, however, that, as individuals, children all progress at different rates.

- Have evidence of any progress that the student has made. It is likely that they have made progress even if it is not in line with age-related expectations.
- Show what the school has done and is continuing to do to support the student.
- Discuss the school's plan to meet the child's needs and what needs to be put in place to support them further.
- Discuss ways that the family can support the child at home.

Keep in mind that most parents just want the best for their child. Depending on your approach, most meetings should be successful in supporting the child to move closer to the goal they need to achieve.

The Solihull Approach (Douglas 2004) also identified three key questions to help parents understand and consequently manage their child's behaviour:

1. What is the exact age and developmental stage of your child? (This may include what are they trying to do at the moment, e.g. learning to crawl, feeding self, overcoming difficulties getting to sleep, going out with their first girlfriend/boyfriend, etc.)
2. What changes have taken place in your lives recently? (Parents need to consider all recent changes, no matter how big or small, e.g. losing a child's favourite cuddly toy, a young person breaking up with their girlfriend/boyfriend.)
3. How well can your child communicate his or her needs to you?

Student-led conferences

These are very effective meetings, switching the focus from the FEO to the student. Students present their behavioural objective to their parents in terms of what they have been learning, what they are good at, what they need to improve on and how they are going to effect those improvements. Parents/carers are encouraged to ask questions; the FEO acts as a 'guide on the side' to offer support or to answer any questions or concerns.

Parents need to be informed about the purpose and benefits of a student-led conference; if this type of meeting is suggested without explanation, parents may gain the impression that the FEO has decided to take a back seat but for the wrong reasons.

Some form of prompt (e.g. a bookmark-style list detailing the structure of the conference) can be given to students to remind them if they forget what they are supposed to do. This is particularly helpful for younger students or those leading a student-led conference for the first time.

A similar resource can be offered to parents including suggestions for questions they might ask their children. This might help particularly early on when parents are not used to this style of meeting.

The question 'Is there something you want to ask me?' can often make parents feel awkward. Give them a helping hand but remind them they are free to ask their own questions.

Most students will not immediately be confident in this style of meeting. They will need modelling, support and lots of practice, as they would with anything new. Make sure they get as much of this as they need before the 'big day' so that they feel enthusiastic and empowered by the experience rather than overwhelmed and daunted.

Focus on what can be achieved

Sometimes it is more productive to acknowledge the negative situation and, instead of focusing on what cannot be changed, focus on what can be changed and, if appropriate, implement the SMART objectives discussed below.

Open discussions

You are more likely to get a parent to open up and reveal their concerns if you ask open questions. This kind of questioning also helps to avoid leading the parent into stating what you assume the problem may be and may instead get you more quickly to the real reason for the problem.

Closed questions might start with 'Did you. . .?' and usually have a 'yes' or 'no' answer.

Open questions usually start with 'What . . .?' 'When . . .?' and 'How . . .?' and require a more detailed response. For example:

- 'How comfortable are you with this plan?'
- 'How could I modify this plan to meet more of your needs?'
- 'What changes have taken place since we last met?'
- 'What information do you need to help with this situation?'
- 'How are you feeling about all of this?'

Setting SMART objectives

SMART is an acronym for the five steps of specific, measurable, achievable, relevant and time-based goals.

- *Specific.* The best goals are well defined and focused. Goal objectives should address the five Ws – who, what, when, where and why. A timeframe for completion is another important specific.
- *Measurable.* Goal objectives should include measures that define quantity and quality. How will the parent and the FEO know when the goal has been successfully met? Focus on elements such as observable actions, quantity and quality to measure outcomes, not activities.
- *Achievable.* A goal objective should be within the parent's/student's power and capabilities, achievable with the available resources and achievable within the stated timeframe. Consider resources, support and home environment support to meet the goal.
- *Relevant.* Goals should meet the parent's/student's needs. Why is the goal important? How will the goal help the parent/student achieve their objectives?
- *Timely.* Goal objectives should identify a specific target date for completion (e.g. by when should this goal be accomplished?) and/or frequencies for specific action steps for achieving the goal (e.g. how often should the parent/student work on these targets?). Incorporate specific dates, calendar milestones or timeframes into the goal objectives.

Once your parent's/student's goals are SMART, break down each goal into a specific set of tasks and activities to accomplish the goals. It's important to review the goals periodically and make adjustments if required. Goal setting is an essential tool for success, especially if your goals are SMART.

Parenting programmes

Evidence is growing that parenting programmes are a cheap and effective use of early intervention resources. Parenting programmes can take many forms but are, in essence, a variety of activities or schemes designed to promote a parent's confidence and develop skills to support their child. Below are some examples of parenting programmes.

The Solihull Approach

The Solihull Approach is an evidence-based theoretical model for working with children and their families, supported by training and comprehensive resource packs. Thousands of the children's workforce are using it across the UK and it has recently been adapted for use in primary schools. It provides a framework for behavioural interventions across a wide range of possible difficulties and leads to professionals making considered choices to help a child to learn and develop effectively. Many schools and children's centres also utilise the Solihull Approach methods and materials for their evidence-based parenting group work on 'Understanding Your Child's Behaviour'. Together they provide a shared understanding for teachers and parents to work together.

In the boroughs where educational psychologists, school nurses and other practitioners are also trained in the Solihull Approach, there are additional advantages to sharing the same language and understanding. The Solihull Approach provides all staff within primary schools an understanding of brain development and how this development takes place within the context of relationships. It introduces the research messages about how children relate and about how they learn to concentrate and control impulsive behaviour. This leads to a greater understanding of how children achieve their academic and social potential and facilitates staff in managing behaviour in the classroom.

Family Values Scheme

The scheme was created and devised specifically to use values to formulate effective partnerships between home and school, and also to enable families to use values to celebrate family life by spending some quality time together. By utilising the Family Values Scheme, teachers and their schools can significantly improve their relationships and communication with parents, raise attendance, reduce bullying and help to nip in the bud potential or actual behavioural problems manifested by their students, either in the early or later stages, with the full knowledge, participation and cooperation of their parents. In order for effective partnerships to be established, the scheme aims for individual families and schools to:

- raise standards in the basic skills of reading and writing;
- strengthen relationships and increase interaction between the family, school and local community;

- use appropriate 'values' to inculcate appropriate standards as an intrinsic way of life both at home and at school;
- improve behaviour and attendance;
- complement and enhance existing personal and social education (PSE) and parental programmes (i.e. by using SEAL);
- raise self-esteem.

(Ellis and Morgan 2009)

The FAST Programme

Families and Schools Together (FAST) is an evidence-based parenting programme that helps children thrive by building strong relationships at home. It was developed in the US by Lynn McDonald, now professor of social work research at Middlesex University.

The FAST programme aims to improve parenting skills and confidence and promote parents' engagement in their child's learning while also improving the behaviour and attendance of their children. The programme is facilitated by accredited FAST trainers, involving teachers and other members of the community, and consists of eight weekly two-and-a-half-hour group sessions.

In groups, families make and share a meal which is served by the children. This is then followed by fun activities involving all family members. During the sessions discussions take place around things such as behaviour management and parenting coaching is provided.

Following the eight sessions, families are involved in monthly refresher sessions led by parents who have completed the programme, which helps to sustain what has been learned.

Incredible Years Programme

The Incredible Years Programme has two related long-term goals. The first is to develop comprehensive treatment programmes for young children with early-onset conduct problems. The second goal is the development of cost-effective, community-based, universal prevention programmes. These are intended for use by families and teachers of young children in order to promote social competence and to prevent children from developing conduct disorders in the first place. The Incredible Years Programme aims to reduce conduct disorders in children by:

- decreasing negative behaviour and non-compliance with parents at home;
- decreasing peer aggression and disruptive behaviour in the classroom.

The programme is also used to promote social, emotional and academic competence in children by increasing:

- children's social skills;
- children's understanding of their own feelings;
- children's conflict self-management skills by decreasing negative attributions;
- children's academic engagement, school readiness and cooperation with teachers.

Family Learning Signature

The Family Learning Signature is a tool designed to help schools improve attainment, attendance and behaviour. It helps families in supporting their child's learning at home as well as strengthening the parent–school relationship. The tool also supports families to work in collaboration to develop solutions that meet their needs.

Strengthening Families

Strengthening Families is an evidence-based 13-week parenting programme covering early years to secondary-age children. The programme is designed for all families including those with complex needs. It is designed to promote protective factors associated with good parenting and better outcomes for children.

The Mellow Parenting Programme

This programme was created to meet the needs of hard-to-reach families and provides parenting support as well as parenting skills. Although research had highlighted that behaviourally based parenting programmes were effective, they were not very successful in recruiting and engaging families from the hard-to-reach category where family and child issues were far more complex, for example:

- mental illness;
- low literacy skills;
- drug/alcohol abuse;
- domestic violence.

Research has shown that when parents attend and complete the Mellow Parenting Programme there is an improvement in:

- mother–child interaction;
- child behaviour problems;
- mother's well-being;
- mother's effectiveness and confidence in parenting.

The Marlborough Model Multiple Family Therapy Groups in Schools

The Marlborough Model is a programme designed for families to help their children who are at risk of exclusion. There are usually six to eight parents in a group, and these groups meet once a week for up to two hours. As well as the school monitoring student behaviour and targets during the sessions with parents, there is a focus on discussing problematic behaviour both at home and in school which enables parents to contribute and share their own good practice. The programme aims to:

- help reduce behaviour that could lead to exclusion;
- develop students' social and emotional skills;

- support parents in developing a healthy relationship with their child and the school;
- encourage parental involvement with mental health professionals;
- share skills and knowledge between mental health and education professionals;
- help raise students' achievement.

Restorative Thinking Parenting Programme (Parenting Without Conflict)

This programme coupled with restorative approaches in school is extremely effective as it aims to help support parents' understanding of their child's behaviour by teaching restorative thinking and skills. The programme is delivered over four two-and-a-half-hour sessions, with groups of family members.

Restorative justice schemes in schools have been started as a result of the drive towards making schools more child-friendly places. The main reason, however, for the development of restorative justice approaches has been because of the need to re-establish relationships following a breakdown, possibly as a result of indiscipline. Some schools, looking for solutions to concerns about indiscipline and disaffection, aggression and violence, now appreciate that there is a need not only to restore good relationships but also to encourage a positive school ethos which reduces the possibilities of further conflicts arising.

The Restorative Thinking Parenting Programme encourages parents to be reflective when looking at their child's behaviour and what the behaviour may be communicating regarding unmet needs. Reflection is also encouraged for parents to consider their own parenting styles, and the programme provides effective skills and awareness to help repair and rebuild relationships.

> Unlike punitive approaches, in which a third party acts as judge, jury and executioner, restorative practice predicates upon ownership of behaviour and conflict resting with those directly involved, who also retain responsibility for resolution of the problem.
>
> (Howard 2009: 5)

Give parents strategies to help their child

Workshops can be organised to help establish why children sometimes don't listen. Sessions can cover the following:

- Set quick boundaries so your child listens the first time.
- Implement effective rules, routines and correctives.
- Engage in positive talk to reduce confrontation.
- Practice six dynamic strategies to deal with unwanted behaviour.
- Learn how to motivate your child using positive reinforcements.

Parent group organisation

To ensure their success, it is key that trained staff are employed to coordinate and deliver parenting programmes. This can either be a designated member(s) of staff from the school or staff from a registered parenting programme.

Co-facilitation works best in terms of initiative, delivery and support. Two facilitators can share the load, manage the dynamics of the group and support each other between sessions. The co-facilitator may be another member of staff; however, a parent who has successfully completed a parenting initiative themselves could also be a co-facilitator, bringing a different perspective and sense of reassurance to the group.

Often, the parents in most need of support have the greatest difficulty in accessing parenting programmes. A variety of factors cause low levels of uptake and high rates of dropout, and these problems are most acute for socially disadvantaged families and parents of children with complex needs. Factors inhibiting access to and successful completion of parenting programmes include:

- lack of information about initiatives;
- fear of stigma or being labelled a 'bad parent';
- a mismatch between the initiative and the parent;
- practical issues such as transport and childcare;
- demands of daily life.

Considerations to take into account when setting up a parenting initiative include:

- identifying parents;
- selecting a venue;
- organising times and dates;
- childcare provision;
- transport provision;
- refreshments.

Identifying parents

It is important to clearly establish the desired outcomes before selecting parents – for example, improving student attendance, behaviour and standards. Once this has been established, invite parents to attend the programme, ensuring that ongoing evaluations take place and that evidence of outcomes is compared at the end of the initiative and/or over an agreed period of time.

Selecting a venue

The venue should be non-threatening and accessible to parents. Consider factors such as local transport and free parking. Although the school might seem an obvious choice, some parents may have negative associations with education or feel stigmatised knowing that the school staff are aware they are attending a parenting initiative.

A more neutral venue such as the local community centre might be more appropriate. In this way, the parents are able to build relationships with other parents. When the time is right, they can encourage and support each other to attend events held at school. The provision of a crÈche may also be a factor in enabling the selected parents to attend.

Organising times and dates

Work commitments and the age of their children are two factors that will determine parents' availability. Before selecting a date and time to run the course, consider:

- coinciding with key events;
- school drop-off and pick-up times;
- school holidays/national holidays;
- parents' work commitments.

It is preferable for the initiatives to fit between major holidays to avoid long gaps which could affect attendance. If possible, have as many sessions as possible before a break to give the group time to gel.

Childcare provision

A crËche may be needed for parents attending the group with younger children. This can be provided by staff at the school, a private company and/or other service providers within the community. Check that the crËche facilities meet the required quality assurance requirements. A planned visit to the crËche before the first session can be helpful for the parent and child so that both become familiar with the environment and with the separation that can sometimes be a cause of anxiety.

Transport provision

Transport to and from the venue needs consideration; some parents may not have access to transport links. The facilitator can either fund transport or arrange pick-ups and drop-offs

Refreshments

Being offered a cup of tea/coffee can help to settle parents and make them feel valued. It helps to start each session with refreshments and, depending on time, also have a break halfway through. If an initiative is taking place after school, consider whether it is necessary to provide food – some parents may have come straight from work.

Attendance

It is important for participants to attend all sessions. Not only will absentees miss out on the content and process of the sessions, but other group members may start to feel that those missing are not part of the group. If someone has missed the first three sessions, it may be better to suggest enrolling them in a later initiative.

The facilitators also need to plan for unforeseen circumstances that would prevent parents from attending (e.g. illness). They should model to the parents that communication and dealing with unforeseen absence are important in terms of the impact that these have on the children.

It is important for the facilitators to establish how they will follow up with non-attendees. For example, ask if parents would like to be telephoned, but make it clear that these are not therapy calls. Include the agreed process in the ground rules established at the first session.

Valuing parents

The professional relationship between the facilitators and parents begins in the very first session and it is crucial to get off to the right start. Remember that the small things matter:

- Establish how the parent would like to be addressed (e.g. Mr Roberts or Paul).
- Remember the parent's name.
- Remember their child(ren)'s name(s).
- Help them feel comfortable and relaxed (e.g. offer them a cup of tea).
- A telephone call from the facilitator before the group starts or, if appropriate, a home visit can make a difference.

Greeting parents as soon as they arrive is important; most people feel nervous attending any session/meeting for the first time, and being met by someone they know will help to put them at ease. Also, don't assume that all parents are literate – signing everyone in can make a big difference to those who feel self-conscious.

Once the session begins, bear in mind that some parents might find the large group daunting and may prefer just to listen rather than participate. Encourage discussions in pairs or smaller groups. The parents' confidence may grow over time and this can then be transferred to large group discussions, as long as the parents are ready for this.

Depending on the group dynamics, it is a good idea to mix each of the smaller groups up so that the same parents are not always in the same group. This ensures that:

- not all quiet parents are in the same group (which may not produce good-quality discussions);
- no 'cliques' are formed and all parents get the opportunity to work with and get to know others;
- parents who have the potential to display unwanted behaviour can be placed in groups to help maintain the desired behaviour.

Before beginning any exercise, inform the parents of the task and the groups they will be working in. This will eliminate any confusion when they start moving around or preparing themselves for a task. Being direct with requests will also help and eliminate any lack of confidence within the group.

Unit 10: Working with parents of children with additional needs

Parents who have children with additional needs can often feel excluded or isolated and therefore need more support and guidance from schools. In some cases many parents take on roles of responsibility – for example, being their child's advocate – and in doing so acquire specialist knowledge of their child's needs which can prove invaluable. It is therefore important that school staff involve parents in their children's learning and the life of the school in ways that will suit their needs. Effective partnerships with home can not only help with the learning and development of the students but also provide parents with support such as helping to clarify administrative and specialist information which parents may receive on a regular basis from other agencies. According to Brian Lamb, author of the Lamb Inquiry on Parental Confidence in Special Educational Needs (2009), the following things are really important to parents:

- appropriate and timely recognition of a child's needs by professionals;
- knowledge and understanding of staff about a child's difficulties and needs;
- the willingness of the service/school to listen to their views and respond flexibly;
- access to specialist services and someone who understands 'my child';
- parents being involved in decision-making about their children and consulted about what services they receive;
- transparent decisions and information about entitlements.

For schools to become inclusive, investment needs to be made to form successful partnerships with parents. Such partnerships are based on taking time to listen to both the school's and parents' points of view in order to address needs and progress with students' learning and well-being. Such partnerships can be challenging, although when organised with the students' outcomes in mind they can prove to be incredibly successful. Section 2 of the *SEND Code of Practice: 0 to 25 Years* (DfE and DoH 2015) has further information on:

- defining parental responsibility;
- key principles in communicating and working in partnership with parents;
- schools working in partnership with parents;
- supporting parents during statutory assessment;
- LEAs working in partnership with parents;
- working in partnership with the voluntary sector;

- parent partnership services;
- preventing and resolving disagreements;
- roles and responsibilities.

All in all, when effective partnerships are formed and sustained, it is the students with additional needs who benefit most from feeling that there is continuity of communication, support and caring between home and school. However, some parents face a multitude of barriers in engaging with school and their child's education. these may include:

- feelings of being excluded and/or isolated;
- suffering from anxiety;
- limited transport to the school;
- their own additional needs;
- caring for another family member;
- feeling apprehensive about what staff and other parents may say;
- being angry about past provision for their child's needs;
- poor experiences with their own schooling;
- feelings of failure based on past experiences.

Staff training

School staff may need additional training when looking to engage parents of students with additional needs in order to create an ethos which is inclusive for all parents. Training to become more skilful in identifying where parents are in terms of their understanding and acceptance of their child's additional need(s) is imperative as some parents may be at different stages on this journey. Some parents may also need extra specialist support. If not available in school, this type of support could be delivered by external agencies and/or specialists such as occupational therapists.

Supporting staff

In order for school staff to effectively support parents, they need to feel supported and fully trained themselves. There are a few ways to help achieve this:

- Have a debrief facility after any serious incident where the staff member(s) involved can talk to a member of the senior leadership team regarding any concerns they may have and what they may have done differently and why.
- Invite a professional into school to talk to staff about a particular additional need (e.g. autism) and provide guidance and strategies to help them support parents.
- Allocate regular slots at staff meetings to enable staff to raise concerns or discuss individual students and/or parents.
- Provide a key member of staff to attend a parent meeting to help support another member of staff.

Clinical supervision

Working with parents whose child has additional needs can be emotionally demanding, but research shows that staff feel more supported when employers provide good clinical supervision on a regular basis. Skills for Care (2007) define 'supervision' as 'an accountable process which supports, assures and develops the knowledge skills and values of an individual group or team'. According to the Care Quality Commission (CQC), this type of supervision provides an opportunity for staff to:

- reflect on and review their practice;
- discuss individual cases in depth;
- change or modify their practice and identify training and continuing development needs.

Understanding improvement

As with any intervention, however small, it can take time before improvement is noticed. Staff need to be aware of this so that they don't lose motivation and purpose. The acronym TIME helps to highlight what is needed in order to see change with parents:

Talk to parents as often as possible, either face-to-face or on the phone.
Invite parents into school or to attend activities in the community.
Mediate immediately to help reduce misunderstandings and rebuild relationships.
Encourage parents, highlighting their knowledge, celebrating their achievements and equipping them with more skills.

Dyslexia-friendly school

The British Dyslexia Association (www.bdadyslexia.org.uk) actively promotes dyslexia-friendly schools to draw awareness to the fact that staff, students and parents learn in different ways. In order to become a dyslexia-friendly school, staff identify the individual learning needs of students and create bespoke types of learning. Support and intervention plans are continually monitored and the school works together to raise awareness of dyslexia and other learning difficulties.

The Family Partnership Model

The Family Partnership Model is an evidence-based model designed to provide a helping process that develops staff skills to enable parents and families to overcome their difficulties. It also builds trust and resilience and develops problem-solving skills. The Family Partnership Model (see Figure 10.1) was developed by Professor Hilton Davis and colleagues from the Centre for Child and Parent Support in London (Day and Davis 2009). Staff learn how to use the model on a five-day training programme; ongoing supervision is an integral aspect of the model (Keatinge *et al.* 2008; Wilson and Huntington 2009).

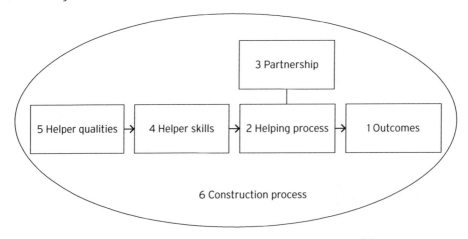

Figure 10.1 The Family Partnership Model

There has been much research carried out on the effectiveness of this model which has highlighted benefits for families of children with intellectual or multiple disabilities living in areas with high rates of poverty (Davis and Rushton 1991) and for families with multiple and complex problems (Davis and Spurr 1998).

Hilton Davis and Lorraine Meltzer, authors of the Department for Education and Skills 2007 publication *Working in Partnership through Early Support*, identified each of the key areas of the family partnership model as follows:

1. Outcomes

In order for the model to be successful, staff must be clear about what they want to achieve. Below are examples.

The outcomes of helping:

- To do no harm.
- To help parents identify, clarify and manage problems.
- To enable parents (including their ability to anticipate problems).
- To enable them to enable the development and well-being of their children.
- To facilitate families' social support and community development generally.
- To enable necessary service support from all agencies.
- To compensate for their difficulties where necessary.
- To change our service systems to become more helpful.

(Davis and Meltzer 2007)

2. The helping process

The helping process outcomes are achieved on a one-to-one basis between parent and member of staff. Below are some examples.

The process of helping:

- Establishing and building a relationship.
- Helping the person explore their current situation.
- Helping them formulate a clearer understanding of the situation.
- Establishing agreed aims and goals.
- Planning strategies.
- Supporting parents while the plans are implemented.
- Evaluating or reviewing the results.
- Ending.

(Davis and Meltzer 2007)

3. Partnership

The partnership provides the ideal type of relationship within this model. Below are examples of the characteristics of an effective partnership.

Characteristics of an effective partnership:

- Working closely together with active participation and involvement.
- Sharing power with parents leading.
- Complementary expertise.
- Agreeing aims and process.
- Negotiation.
- Mutual trust and respect.
- Openness and honesty.
- Clear communication.

(Davis and Meltzer 2007)

4. Helper skills

After defining the outcomes in part one, the process of helping in part two and the partnership relationship in part three, part four looks at the skills needed by the helper to establish and secure the partnership through developing helper skills. Below are a few examples.

Helper skills:

- Attention/active listening.
- Prompting and exploration.
- Empathic responding.
- Summarising.
- Enabling change.
- Negotiating.
- Problem solving.

(Davis and Meltzer 2007)

5. Helper qualities

The next part in the model is ensuring the member of staff has the right qualities in order to achieve parts one to four. Below are a few examples.

Helper qualities:

- Respect.
- Empathy.
- Genuineness.
- Humility.
- Quiet enthusiasm.
- Personal integrity.
- Technical knowledge.

(Davis and Meltzer 2007)

6. Construction process

The final part of the model is an understanding that everyone's 'map of the world' is different and therefore members of staff should refrain from making assumptions that could distort their view of the parent they are working with. Below are a few examples of the assumptions sometimes made.

Construing:

- All people construct a model of the world in their heads.
- This enables people to anticipate and adapt to whatever happens to them.
- The model is derived from their past experience.
- Each person has a unique set of constructions that may overlap with others.
- Constructions are not necessarily conscious or able to be verbalised.
- Constructions are constantly being tested, potentially clarified and changed.
- Social interaction is determined by our constructions of each other.

(Davis and Meltzer 2007)

Communication

Strong home–school communication and partnerships can help to alleviate most of the underlying concerns parents may have regarding their child's education and help eliminate any worries and anxieties that may arise during the academic year. Keeping communication channels open and accessible is therefore key. Although there are many ways parents can communicate with schools without physically being there (see Unit 2), the SEND Code of Practice 2015 requires the SENCO (Special Educational Needs Coordinator) to meet parents face-to-face on a termly basis to discuss the student's progress.

Face-to-face

Where possible information should be given face-to-face with parents to eliminate misunder-standing and also for school staff to show and provide support. The words we use sometimes aren't nearly as important as the tone of voice and body language. According to Mehrabian (1972), there are basically three elements in any face-to-face communication – words, tone of voice and body language – and these three elements contribute differently to the meaning of the message. Words account for 7 per cent, tone of voice accounts for 38 per cent and body language accounts for 55 per cent. Face-to-face communication is therefore very important when dealing with sensitive issues so that all areas of our communication are aligned.

Asking open questions

When working with parents and, in some cases, discussing sensitive issues, using open questions can have many advantages as they encourage authentic responses and two-way communication, helping to develop a professional working relationship. Table 10.1 provides a few examples.

Open questions can start with 'why', 'what', 'when', 'where', 'who' and 'how'. Below are some examples of open questions which can be used during a meeting with a parent.

- What can you tell me about (child's name)?
- What can we do to help (child's name) to settle into his new class?
- What types of activity is (child's name) interested in?
- What makes (child's name) feel happy?
- What does (child's name) enjoy most about school?
- What does (child's name) find challenging?
- What concerns do you have about (child's name) coming to school?
- What changes have you noticed since (child's name) started in his new class?
- How would you like us to keep you informed regarding how (child's name) is doing?
- How confident are you that we are doing enough to meet (child's name) needs?

> People don't care how much you know until they know how much you care!
>
> (Theodore Roosevelt)

Delivering sensitive news

According to Buckman (1992), bad news is defined as 'any information which adversely and seriously affects an individual's view of his or her future'. The impact of sensitive news differs

Table 10.1 Examples of open and closed questions

Open questions	Closed questions
Ask the parent to think and reflect	Give facts
Encourage enhanced levels of cooperation and understanding	Are quick to answer
Give opinions and feelings	Require a yes or no answer
Encourage the parent's ideas, concerns and feelings	Can be asked to identify a certain piece of information
Share what is present for the parent	
Show respect and interest in others	

according to the parent receiving it as well as their expectations or understanding of their child's additional need(s). However, bad news or sensitive news always needs to be delivered in a tactful way. Baile *et al.* (2000) devised SPIKES, a six-step protocol for delivering bad news. Below is an adaptation of this.

Step 1: **S** – *Setting up the meeting*

This involves the member of staff who is to deliver the news being mentally prepared, relaxed and composed. Creating the right environment, which is relaxed but also provides the right level of privacy, also needs to be planned. It is also important to understand that although what is being delivered to the parent may be of concern, 'the information may be important in allowing them to plan for the future' (Baile *et al.* 2000).

Step 2: **P** – *Assessing the **parent's** perception*

Gaining an understanding of the parent's perception and understanding regarding their child is important. This is where asking open questions has a big advantage in gaining an accurate picture, for example 'What have you been told about your child's diagnosis?' This information will give the member of staff an indication of where the parent is at and, if needed, allow them to correct any misinterpretations they may have.

Step 3: **I** – *Obtaining the parent's **invitation***

Although some parents may want to gain more information regarding their child's additional needs, others may be in denial or just coming to terms with a diagnosis. If the latter, the member of staff can ask the following questions to gain a better understanding of the best way to deliver the information:

> 'What is the best way for me to give you the information?'
> 'Would you like a friend or family member to sit with you and support you during this meeting?'
> 'Would you prefer to ask questions in order to receive the information?'

Step 4: **K** – *Giving **knowledge** and information to the parent*

In order to prepare the parent for the news, give them an indication beforehand that bad or sensitive news is on its way. This will help the parent process the information more easily. Using the same language as the parent and avoiding unnecessary jargon will also help.

Step 5: **E** – *Address the parent's **emotions** with **empathic** responses*

Parents' emotional reactions to receiving bad and/or sensitive news can vary greatly and the member of staff needs to be prepared in order to make the necessary empathetic response. Parents' emotional responses can range from anger and silence to denial and crying. Asking open questions and showing the parent empathy and understanding goes a long way to help calm the situation. It is only when the situation is calm that step 6 can be implemented.

Step 6: **S** *- Strategy and* **summary**

When parents are clear about a way forward regarding their child, they become less anxious and uncertain. Devising a plan may need to take place at a different time if the parent is not ready. The discussion regarding a way forward should also include the involvement of the parent so that there is a shared responsibility for decision-making. This will allow the parent to feel more in control and that they are positively contributing to their child's progress.

A place to talk

Provide a room within the school where parents can talk in confidence regarding any concerns they may have about their child's additional need(s). The room should be comfortable and inviting, a place where staff create a respectful and relaxing atmosphere for all so that parents can talk about matters that concern them.

The handbook

Providing a handbook full of information for parents can be useful in helping to reduce anxiety and isolation. The handbook can include the following:

- names, contact details and photos of designated staff within the school;
- key information on transitions;
- information on how the school communicates with parents;
- services available within the community and school;
- list of relevant agencies, helplines, support groups and charities;
- top tips compiled by other parents.

DVD communication

This is a creative and accessible form of communication which provides parents with a regular DVD of their child's learning and achievements. The DVD can show parents their child's achievements with examples of their work, information on what they are learning and an insight into their well-being. The DVD can be introduced by the class teacher and also the student. This provides a great communication tool, especially for parents with learning difficulties or parents who rarely engage with school.

Case study: Charlton Park Academy - multimedia advocacy

Charlton Park Academy is a successful, oversubscribed secondary special academy in Greenwich that offers a high-quality educational experience and an individualised approach to education to students with complex, low-incidence special educational needs.

   The school believes it is essential that everyone has a comprehensive understanding of each student so it has adopted a multimedia advocacy approach and simple, web-based tools called RIX Wikis to ensure that everyone living and working with a child or young person with learning disabilities can communicate and share information effectively.

Too often, the focus can be on the limitations placed on a child or young person by their disability. In contrast, the RIX Wiki shows the person and not the 'label'. The focus is positive, highlighting their strengths, goals and achievable outcomes. The Wiki can help build a detailed picture of who they really are as people – what and who is important to them, what they like to do, how they communicate and how they see their future.

This step-change in support for the students at Charlton Park Academy is a progressive response to new legislation. In September 2014, the Government introduced the biggest education reforms in a generation for children and young people (CYP) with special educational needs and disabilities (SEND). The SEND reforms position CYP at the heart of planning and decision-making. Support professionals need to work together with CYP and their families to put the education, health and care (EHC) plans into place through person-centred practice.

Prior to the reforms coming into effect, 'Pathfinder' teams around the country took part in pilots. The Royal Borough of Greenwich Pathfinder team commissioned a pilot of RIX Wikis at Charlton Park Academy. RIX Wikis are simple, secure, web-based multimedia tools which very effectively support EHC planning by embedding a multimedia advocacy approach. The pilot aimed to evaluate the effectiveness of the new technology and multimedia advocacy approaches on person-centred planning (PCP).

Staff and students from Charlton Park Academy, parents, carers, the Greenwich Pathfinder Project team and RIX Research & Media collaborated in the pilot which ran from April 2012 until March 2013.

The results were conclusive. PCP using multimedia advocacy showed a 93 per cent increase in the awareness of PCP where plans were set up within the experimental group. There was a 0 per cent increase within the control group.

Multimedia advocacy enabled over 50 per cent of the students to understand their plans more than they did before the pilot. Within the experimental group, 78 per cent more members from the circle of support contributed to the student's person-centred plan when using the multimedia advocacy approach. The approach was also found to help capture the difficult communication of some students and improve behaviour.

In 2014/15, Charlton Park Academy fully adopted multimedia advocacy and now uses RIX Wikis for all 240 of the pupils in the school. The Wikis have produced genuinely positive outcomes for the students and their families. Students enjoy greater independence, increased self-advocacy, better engagement and boosted self-confidence. The Wikis have improved the home–school partnership and support parents, teachers and health professionals in communicating and collaborating effectively by sharing a wide range of information. In 2015, Ofsted twice cited RIX Wikis in the inspection report for the school:

> Residential care plans now include an explanation of how staff are to engage and ensure that they plan care to include students and that plans are as accessible as possible. The school has exceeded this suggestion in the development of safe online individual forums, called 'wikis', for sharing plans and achievements. These

student-led and created websites have enabled grandparents living overseas to also share in the celebrations of residential students' progress. This technology and empowering process gives control of plans to residential students and means that students can define their own identity, hopes and aspirations.

Wikis are person-centred and empowering, as students can share information, express themselves and celebrate their progress and achievements in a safe way.

Learning

Getting to know your child

Invite parents into school to create a 'getting to know my child' book to enable staff to gain more of an understanding regarding the student they'll be working with. Ask parents to include the following:

- photographs of their child from birth to present age;
- photographs of members of the family;
- their child's likes and dislikes;
- pieces of work created by their child;
- tickets, programmes, etc. from activities/events their child has attended;
- five interesting facts about their child.

Friendship groups

Parents always want to know how their child is socialising with others and who they are friends with. Update parents on a regular basis regarding their child's friendship group. This may also encourage play dates resulting from parents contacting other parents.

Home-school diary

A paper or electronic home–school diary is important not only for parents to gain an insight into their child's day but also for staff to ascertain any issues or events from home that could potentially impact on the student's day. Depending on the parents' needs, the diary can be structured in a number of different ways – for example, with photos, checklists, audio, etc. This is also an excellent way to get parents to contribute to their child's record-keeping.

Visual timetable

Using visual support strategies such as visual timelines helps to remind students about their daily routines both in school and at home. Support parents in making a visual timetable either by inviting them into school or by uploading a step-by-step DVD guide on to the school website. Show parents how to use symbols to represent the activities or lessons their child will attend. These are then selected and displayed on the timetable to show what is going to happen, including which member of their family will be picking them up at the end of the day. See https://uk.pinterest.com/nsmtraining/engaging-families for more ideas.

Inform parents of the many benefits of making such a timetable, such as:

- reducing their child's anxiety;
- simplifying the concepts of before, after, first, next, morning, afternoon, evening;
- using a different form of communication;
- providing their child with a clear structure to their day;
- building upon their child's need for routine;
- promoting their child's independence.

Home learning

Helping parents to support their child at home by providing information, guidelines, resources and activities not only provides a structure but also leaves the parent feeling supported. Provide top tips, ideas and resources to inspire parents to help their child's learning and wellbeing in a fun and enjoyable way. This provides regular feedback and acknowledgement of how well they are doing and celebrates their successes.

Home learning can involve:

- providing growth mindset praise (see Unit 8);
- supporting homework (see Unit 8);
- attending workshops to gain practical information to help support learning at home;
- taking part in family reading time (see Unit 8);
- participating in schemes such as the Family Values Scheme – the Scheme provides a variety of activities and tasks for families to complete at home (see Unit 8).

Support

Signposting

Finding the right support can be very challenging for some parents, so schools can help to reduce the confusion and stress by signposting parents. Schools have access to a range of services and activities available in the community as well as more specialised interventions such as social services, educational psychologists, speech and language therapy. Local authorities provide Parent Partnership Services which are designed to provide support and advice to parents of children with special educational needs (SEN). Provision can be found by contacting the National Parent Support Network or the local council. Services include:

- confidential telephone helpline;
- information and advice on SEN issues;
- support in preparing for and attending meetings;
- contact details for local support groups;
- support and guidance when completing forms.

Families were signposted to a variety of services within the local area including benefits support, housing advice, carers centre, Family Fund, debt advice, after-school activities. Support was given to those families who found it difficult to access these services. Support to attend hospital appointments and other relevant appointments was also given.

(St Giles School, South Croydon, Surrey)

Designated member of staff

Some parents may need additional support, including home visits. Having a designated member of staff within the school to work with and support parents is key. Unit 3 looks at the role of the family engagement officer.

Multi-agency involvement

Multi-agency involvement offers a range of services and support for parents including Team Around the Child (TAC) meetings, Team Around the Family (TAF) meetings, Pastoral Support Programme (PSP) meetings, Child in Need (CIN) meetings and SEN Support Reviews, as well has having involvement with parenting support programmes and other interventions. See Unit 9 for more information.

> Due to the nature of the needs of the students, multi-agency working was essential. The school had a large Multi-Disciplinary Team from the local health authority working within school and working closely together to meet the needs of students and their families, recognising that these partnerships are vital to enable students to access the curriculum offered within school.
>
> (St Giles School, Croydon, Surrey)

Support groups

Organise coffee mornings to provide opportunities for parents to network and socialise with others so that they can share experiences and provide each other support. If needed, introduce a buddy system (see Unit 7).

Information fairs

During the academic year schools can hold themed information fairs and workshops for parents. These can take on different themes throughout the year such as autism awareness, positive behaviour management, speech and language. Key speakers can be invited as well as community support projects to provide a varied session to benefit all.

Workshops

Providing workshop within school and the community of specialised subjects can help build parents' confidence and skill sets. Workshops can include:

- Makaton language programme;
- Understanding sign language;

- PECS (picture exchange communication system);
- Practical behaviour management strategies;
- Understanding the adolescent brain;
- Supporting your child with attachment difficulties.

Champion a speaker

Many parents over the years have undoubtedly specialised in their child's additional need(s), acquiring invaluable information and knowledge. Ask parents to share their expertise by organising an evening with a key speaker specialising in a certain area such as autism. The parent can choose to introduce the speaker and also chair a question-and-answer session where they can impart their own personal experience and information from a parent point of view to benefit others.

Transitions

Transitions are times of change which can be very stressful for students with additional needs as well as their parents. Research conducted by Dunlop and Fabian (2007) suggests that the way in which a student's first transitions are handled could potentially have a significant impact on the child's capacity to cope with change in the short and long term. Therefore time and planning needs to be invested not only with the student but also with the parent to ensure that the transition is well managed and so that the student doesn't feel isolated and vulnerable. Below are some suggested ways to help support the parent and student in this process:

- Organise a presentation evening to inform parents of the transition process. For those parents who are unable to attend, arrange a home visit.
- Update the school website with information, resources, timetable examples, designated member of staff, map and/or virtual tour of the school.
- Find out if there is a 'safe place' where your child can go if they feel worried or if there is a particular member of staff they can talk to.
- Invite parents to a workshop to create a passport for their child. The passport can include necessary information about them, their needs, behaviour, communication styles, all of which can provide staff with essential information until they get to know the student.
- Provide parents with information to help their child get into good routines (e.g. sleep) before the first day of term.
- Invite parents to accompany their child into class for a lesson so that they can gain an understanding of what and how their child is learning.
- Provide parents with a checklist regarding what they need for their child, the checklist can include:
    - map of the school;
    - timetable of the school day;

- information on how their child will be made to feel welcome;
- copy of the school calendar listing all key meetings and events;
- list of after-school clubs;
- contact details of designated teacher;
- information given to class teacher regarding the specific needs of their child;
- successful strategies staff can use with their child;
- types of support their child will receive;
- meeting dates before and after the key points of transition;
- a list of questions parents may want to ask at the meeting;
- a list of resources their child will need at their new school;
- how to create a transition board with photos of the school, key rooms, new staff, school uniform, etc. to help prepare the child for their transition;
- advice on a seating plan which best fits their child.

Case Study: Transition at St Giles School

A comprehensive transition programme at St Giles School was put in place to ensure smooth transitions into school at Reception age. Their aim was to begin 'early interactions to build positive relationships'. Typically, this was the largest area of transition and was currently being extended to all transitions into school across all age ranges.

Transition into Reception typically began as soon as pupils were identified by the local authority. Visits were made to current settings and the school worked jointly with the local authority Early Support Team. Due to the high level of pupils' needs, transition meetings were arranged with families and all professionals involved with the child to ensure a smooth transition.

Families were also invited into school during the summer term for a 'new families' meeting where they had a chance to meet their child's class teacher and receive information that helped in the transition process.

Home visits were carried out in the new term prior to starting school to ensure any changes over the summer holiday (possibly medical/developmental) were taken into account. The family support worker liaised closely with class staff and families during the new term to ensure that any queries or concerns were dealt with as and when they arose. This process also identified families who needed further support.

Transitions policy

Having a well-established transition policy provides guidance and expectations to enable an effective transition process not only for students but also for parents. Have a 'transition champion' who is responsible for supporting both students and parents and to provide that extra level of support. Below is an example of a transition policy from Fairlands Primary School and Nursery.

Fairlands Primary School and Nursery Transition Policy

'is a process, not an event'

Our vision

To provide a secure, happy and stimulating environment for all where extended learning opportunities are provided to develop emotionally, socially and intellectually.

Introduction

In this policy 'transition' describes the movement that takes place from one familiar setting (including the home) to another. Care and attention is given to each stage for an individual, groups or cohorts of children to, through and beyond Fairlands Primary School.

Aims

We want our children to experience a smooth educational and emotional transition throughout their learning to ensure that all children continue to make the very best progress.

Equal opportunities and inclusion

- Staff, children, parents, governors and other agencies are actively involved in the process and their perceptions about transition are explored and valued.
- Measures are taken to ensure all children are given the opportunity to experience a similar ease of transition.

Principles

- Approaches to teaching and learning are harmonised at the point of transition.
- Planning is based upon assessment information from the previous class/setting.
- Styles of teaching and learning meet the needs of the children and not preconceived notions of what is appropriate for the next phase/key stage.
- There is a professional regard for the information from the previous setting/class.
- Children are able to enjoy new approaches at transition.
- Transition motivates and challenges children.
- Staff allocation gives particular attention to the particular needs of the children.
- Effective transition takes time and is a process rather than an event.
- Transitions are not overlooked or left to chance but thought about and planned in advance.
- Feedback from children and parents is encouraged and valued.

Practice

Transition from Pre-School to the Nursery

- Parents are invited to a 'New to Nursery' meeting which is used as an opportunity to introduce parents to staff and our Family Lives worker.

- 'Tea and Tissues' sessions are run by the Family Lives worker for the week of new nursery starters to reassure anxious parents.
- Parents and children receive a home visit.
- Parents receive an information pack.
- Staggered induction of children over the first week.
- Children receive a pre-school visit (observation/information sharing).
- Pre-schools receive a Fairlands school uniform and book bag for their role-play area.
- Children are invited to use the Nursery lunch club.
- Children spend a session with their new teaching team.
- Fairlands Pre-school bring their children over to Fairlands Nursery for a session.
- A 'Passport to Nursery' is given to all children before they start at the school.
- Parents are invited into the Nursery for up to an hour on their first day.
- Nursery children make a 'What happens in Nursery?' book for the next Nursery class.
- Early in the summer term the SENCO visits Fairlands pre-school and other pre-school settings where children with SEN are identified.
- New teachers spend planned time in the Foundation Stage over the summer term, where possible.

Transition from Nursery to Reception

- Parents are invited to a 'New to Reception' meeting which is used as an opportunity to introduce parents to staff and our Family Lives worker.
- 'Tea and Tissues' sessions are run on the first day of term to reassure anxious parents.
- Parents and children new to the school receive a home visit.
- Parents receive an information pack.
- Children new to the school receive a visit (observation/information sharing) to their previous setting.
- Children spend a session with their new teaching team.
- Children attend half days for the first week.
- All Reception staff stay with them at lunchtime for the first few weeks.
- A 'Passport to Reception' is given to all children before they start at the school.
- The final topic in the summer term explores issues of change.
- Children make a 'What happens in Reception?' book for the next Reception class.
- New teachers spend planned time in the Foundation Stage over summer term, where possible.
- Parents are invited to record both theirs and their child's feelings on the transition form sent home.
- In the autumn term, the provision closely reflects summer term practice in Nursery.

Transition from the Foundation Stage to Year 1

- Parents and children new to the school receive a home visit.
- Parents and children new to the school visit the school, meet staff and receive an information pack.
- Children write a letter to their new teacher.
- Reception visit the current Year 1 for a shared picnic in the second half of the summer term.
- Cohort visit new classes and teaching team.
- In the autumn term, the provision closely reflects summer term practice in Reception.
- Start-of-day procedures for Year 1 are rehearsed by Reception children in the last two weeks of the summer term, i.e. lining up in Year 1 playground.

Transition from Year 1 to Year 2

- Parents and children new to the school receive a home visit.
- Parents and children new to the school visit the school, meet staff and receive an information pack.
- Children write a letter to their new teacher.
- Throughout Year 1 there are staggered changes to provision to ensure a smooth transition to Year 2.
- Start of day procedures for Year 2 are rehearsed by Year 1 children in the last six weeks of the summer term, i.e. entrance through statue gate.
- In the summer term, additional opportunities are created for shared breaks, playtimes and cross-site events to familiarise Year 1 children with upper site and teaching staff.
- Literacy and maths books and guided reading records are passed up from Year 1 to 2.
- Handover meetings are held in the summer term.
- 'New to . . . Meetings' are held in the summer term.

Transition in subsequent Years (2–6) throughout the school

- Parents and children new to the school receive a home visit.
- Parents and children new to the school visit the school and meet their teacher.
- Meet the teacher session in new classroom in the summer term.
- All 'New to Year __' welcome meetings take place in the summer term.
- Curriculum information booklets for the first half-term are given to parents at this meeting.
- All year groups take part in a transition unit of work in the summer term, which is picked up in the autumn term.
- Class rules and helping hands completed in first week.

- Literacy, maths, RE and art sketch books are passed up with the child. Children continue working in these books in September.
- Handover meetings are held in the summer term. The following information should be passed on/made available to the next teacher:
  - Reading book band colour
  - Individual reading records
  - Inclusion files
  - Medical records – generated from SIMS by School Office
  - Highlighted Steps sheets
  - Access to CPOMS records
  - Literacy and maths books – current book for all core subjects for every child AND HOLD ON TO EVERYTHING for one high, one middle, one lower attaining child, from each class. This is for Ofsted purposes.
  - Sketch books
  - RE books
  - MFL folders/books
  - Learning support records
  - Learn-it record
  - Class summary sheet

In-year admissions from Nursery to Year 6

- Parents and children new to the school visit the school to meet staff.
- Parents receive an information pack.
- Parents and children new to the school receive a home visit, where slides from the relevant 'New to Year _' meeting are shared.
- Previous setting contacted for all pupils.
- Children with SEN: SENCO contacts previous setting and may visit to receive information.
- Records from previous setting made available to class teacher and SENCO.
- Children are given a buddy from within the class.
- A letter is sent to the previous school requesting any safeguarding or child protection information.

Children leaving from Nursery to Year 6

- Parents are invited to a meeting with the head teacher.
- All records are passed on promptly including safeguarding records.
- Children with SEN – information shared by phone or through a visit from the SENCO if transferring settings locally.
- Relevant child protection information is transferred on.

Transition from Year 6 to Year 7		
Summer of Year 5	*Autumn of Year 6*	*Summer of Year 6*
A transition support meeting/group with Family Lives worker is offered to parents in the summer term of Year 5, in preparation for starting Year 6 and choosing secondary schools.	Children visit their secondary school open evenings. Children choose their secondary schools.	Children attend a secondary transfer day. Children work on a transition unit of work - Passport to Secondary School. SENCO arranges extra visits for vulnerable children. Behaviour TA runs 'Our Time' transition group for vulnerable children. Class teachers and SENCO meet staff of receiving secondary schools. SENCO prepares SEN records for transfer. Class teachers and SENCO meet staff of receiving secondary schools. End of year reports and SATs results sent on to secondary schools. Common transfer files completed and sent to secondary schools. Relevant child protection files are transferred on.

Children moving families

- The Designated Teacher for Looked After Children (DTCLA) to work alongside social worker to implement their transition plan, e.g. to host meetings between prospective adoptive parents and school staff.

Vulnerable children

- Children with specific medical or educational needs have individual transition plans. These are organised and supported by the SENCO.

Review

The Governing Body will review this policy in line with its annual cycle of review.

Planning

Involving parents in the school's planning process regarding their child's education is integral to promoting inclusion for all and empowering parents to achieve their goals and aspirations for their child. Planning should be person-centred, where the school puts the child and family at the centre of the planning process so that they can plan aspects of their well-being and learning. Also involved in the person-centred planning can be community support teams, social workers, etc. Planning can also involve:

- auditing engagement with parents (see Unit 1);
- including parental engagement as a regular agenda item at staff meetings;

- reviewing action plans on a regular basis in partnership with parents (see Unit 1);
- consulting parents in reviews, planning, evaluation and decision-making;
- updating parents on the new SEN code of practice;
- encouraging parents to drive school improvement, assessment and service delivery;
- involving parents in the planning and organisation of transitions;
- collecting parent views regarding provision in order to compile an effective parent involvement policy (see the example below).

Parent views regarding SEN provision

All parents should be given a questionnaire, regardless of whether or not their child is on the SEN register.

Please tick	Strongly agree	Agree	Disagree	Strongly disagree
The school caters for my child's needs				
My child is given work appropriate for his/her ability				
The school has high expectations for my child				
The school keeps me informed about my child's progress and what he/she should be doing next to improve				
The school gives appropriate support to children and young people with SEN				
Children and young people with SEN make good progress				
The school deals with any concerns I may have about my child's progress				
I am aware of the school's SEN policy				
I know how to obtain more information about the SEN policy				

Please tick	Always	Usually	Sometimes	Never
Information about my child's progress is clear and helpful				
My child feels challenged by the work he/she does				
My child knows who to ask if he/she needs help				

Evaluating parent perception (SEN)

Please tick	Strongly agree	Agree	Disagree	Strongly disagree
This school has high expectations for my child				
The school caters for my child's needs				
I am confident that my child is making the best progress				
My child is given work appropriate for his/her ability				
The school gives my child the support he/she needs to make progress				
The school keeps me informed of any additional support my child receives				
The school keeps me informed about my child's progress				
The school deals with any concerns I may have about my child's progress				

Please tick	Always	Usually	Sometimes	Never
I am involved in discussions about my child's needs				
Information about my child's progress is clear and helpful				
My child is given homework appropriate for his/her needs				
My child feels well supported				

Any additional comments:

Additional support

The next section is for parents of children receiving additional support from an external agency.

My child receives additional support from: ....

Please tick	Very good	Good	OK	Poor
How would you describe the effectiveness of the extra support your child receives?				
How would you describe the information you receive about the additional support your child receives?				
What does your child think about the extra support he/she receives?				
Please include any additional comments about the support your child receives:				

The next section is for parents of children with a statement of SEN.

How do you feel about . . . (please tick)	Very happy	Happy	OK	Unhappy
The provision at the setting in relation to your child's SEN?				
Your involvement in review meetings and planning meetings?				
The information you receive?				
Your child's statement?				
Please include any additional comments about the support your child receives:				

Resources

Additional needs

Afasic
A charity for children and young adults with communication impairments.
www.afasic.org.uk

British Dyslexia Association
Campaigns and provides support to break down barriers and enable dyslexic people to reach their potential.
www.bdadyslexia.org.uk

British Institute of Learning Disabilities (BILD)
Provides people with learning disabilities with the right kind of support so they can make choices and decisions about the things that affect their lives.
www.bild.org.uk

Contact a Family
UK-wide charity providing advice, information and support to the parents of all disabled children.
www.cafamily.org.uk

Dyspraxia Foundation
Committed to making the teaching and medical professions more aware of dyspraxia and to spreading understanding of how those who have the condition can be helped.
www.dyspraxiafoundation.org.uk

Epilepsy Action
Campaigns to improve epilepsy services and to raise awareness of the condition.
www.epilepsy.org.uk

Face2Face parent befriending (Scope)
A network of trained volunteer befrienders who can help parents make positive adjustments to the news that their child has a disability.
www.scope.org.uk/support/services/befriending

I Can

The national educational charity for special schools, nurseries and centres within local schools. Provides training and information for parents, teachers and therapists.
www.ican.org.uk

Information, Advice and Support Services Network (IASS Network)

Provides training and support to local Information Advice and Support Services across England. The IASS Network was previously known as the National Parent Partnership Network (NPPN), which undertook a similar role with local Parent Partnership Services.
www.iassnetwork.org.uk

National Autistic Society

Provides individuals with autism and their families with help, support and services.
www.nas.org.uk

National Children's Bureau (NCB)

Provides training, conferences and consultancy for children and families.
www.ncb.org.uk

National Portage Association

A home-visiting educational service for pre-school children with additional support needs and their families.
www.portage.org.uk

Awards and parent associations

Investors in Families Award

A quality mark that recognises the work that schools and other settings undertake with families to improve outcomes for children and young people. The quality mark is awarded to schools and other settings that demonstrate a commitment to working with families. IIF Wales is a national scheme, with national standards, that is accredited locally.
https://iifwales.com

Leading Parent Partnership Awards

A national award that provides a coherent framework through which schools, early years settings and other educational organisations can deliver effective parental engagement from early years to post-16.
www.lppa.co.uk

Parent Councils UK

Information and resources on how to set up a parent council in school.
www.parentcouncils.co.uk

PTA UK

A charity designed to encourage positive cooperation between home and school. The site also includes information on how to set up a Parent Teacher Association within the school.
www.pta.org.uk

Health and well-being

Action for Children

Provides parenting advice, a safe space for families to play and the chance to learn new skills, subjects and information. The centres also help practically, with things like debt and housing difficulties, and offer self-help or family therapy for problems such as sexual abuse, domestic violence and anti-social behaviour.
www.actionforchildren.org.uk

Bibliotherapy

Most local authorities offer a Child and Family Bibliotherapy Scheme. These include self-help books recommended by specialists. This recommended book will be available through their local library. The recommended books can be viewed here:
www.nhsdirect.wales.nhs.uk/lifestylewellbeing/bibliotherapy

CAMHS (Child and Adolescent Mental Health Services)

Provides help and treatment for children and young people with emotional, behavioural and mental health difficulties.
www.nhs.uk/NHSEngland/AboutNHSservices/mental-health-services-explained/

Families Anonymous

Helping those who have someone they care about who is using drugs.
www.famanon.org.uk

Family Lives

A charity with over three decades of experience helping parents to deal with the changes that are a constant part of family life.
http://familylives.org.uk

Mind

Provides advice and support to empower anyone experiencing a mental health problem.
www.mind.org.uk

Young Minds

Provides information and advice on the emotional well-being and health of children and young people.
www.youngminds.org.uk

Multicultural groups

British Council
Supports adults in learning English.
http://learnenglish.britishcouncil.org/en/

Supports teenagers in learning English.
http://learnenglishteens.britishcouncil.org/

Supports children in learning English.
http://learnenglishkids.britishcouncil.org/en/

Little Bridge
An online programme to help children and parents learn English.
www.littlebridge.com

Reciteme
Software to translate websites into other languages.
www.reciteme.com

Scottish Association of Minority Ethnic Educators (SAMEE)
Empowers and supports minority ethnic educators to realise their individual aspirations and progress their career in the Scottish education system.
www.samee.org.uk

Stonewall
Stonewall's campaign against homophobic bullying provides information and support.
www.stonewall.org.uk

Parenting programmes and initiatives

Department for Education
Find a parenting programme.
www.education.gov.uk/commissioning-toolkit/Programme/ParentsSearch

Family Links – Nurturing Programme
An emotional and mental health programme designed to strengthen family relationships, aimed at parents of children aged 2–15 at universal and targeted levels of need.
www.familylinks.org.uk

Family Values Scheme
A simple yet effective way of engaging families including the 'hard to reach'. The Family Values Scheme is based around a set of 22 values designed to encourage families to participate

in a series of fun tasks and challenges which they plan and carry out together in their own home and/or educational setting.
www.nsmtc.co.uk

Incredible Years Programmes

For parents of children aged 0-6 years. Can be offered universally and as targeted programmes for a range of child behaviour and attention problems. The programme aims to promote protective factors such as positive and nurturing parenting, school involvement and positive family and peer support, while reducing risk factors.
http://incredibleyears.com

Marlborough Model Multiple Family Therapy Groups in Schools

Central and North West London NHS Foundation Trust.
www.cnwl.nhs.uk

National Parent Council

Information on how to set up a Parent Association in your school.
www.npc.ie

Nurture Group Network

Raises the profile of nurture; takes its agenda to the heart of government, enabling access to nurture provision for all.
http://nurturegroups.org

The Playclub Project

Provides fun, imaginative learning activities for families to do at home which raise attainment.
www.playbags.co.uk

Solihull Approach Parenting Programme

Courses in understanding your child's behaviour can be undertaken in face-to-face groups and are for all parents and carers: mothers, fathers, partners and grandparents.
www.solihullapproachparenting.com

Strengthening Families Strengthening Communities

A programme designed to reduce child behavioural difficulties and help parents build child self-esteem, aimed at parents of children aged 3-18 at universal and targeted levels of need.
www.strengthening-families.org.uk

Parent support

Barnardos

Provides support for parents and children.
www.barnardos.org.uk

Family Action - Building Stronger Families
A leading provider of services to disadvantaged and socially isolated families.
www.family-action.org.uk

Family Lives
Online parenting and family support.
http://familylives.org.uk

Gingerbread
Provides expert advice and practical support, and campaigns for single parents.
www.gingerbread.org.uk

Grandparents' Association
A national charity which supports all grandparents and their families.
www.grandparents-association.org.uk

Home-Start
A national family support charity that helps parents to build better lives for their children. Volunteers provide support and friendship to more than 32,000 families every year.
www.home-start.org.uk

Net Mums
Provides online parenting advice and information.
www.netmums.com

One Parent Families Scotland
Provides help to all single-parent families: mums, dads, young parents and kinship carers.
www.opfs.org.uk

Working Families
The UK's leading work-life balance organisation. Helps working parents and carers and their employers to find a better balance between responsibilities at home and work.
www.workingfamilies.org.uk

Parenting support for dads

Families Need Fathers
A charity chiefly concerned with supporting all parents, dads, mums and grandparents to have personal contact and meaningful relationships with children following parental separation.
https://fnf.org.uk

Fatherhood Institute
The UK's fatherhood think-and-do-tank designed to provide children with a strong positive relationship with their father.
www.fatherhoodinstitute.org

Fathers Network Scotland
Provides support, resources and events for dads.
www.fathersnetworkscotland.org.uk

Including Men
Brings together support and resources for early years, learning and family services.
www.includingmen.com

Parent surveys

Education Survey & Research Service (EdSRS)
Provides a comprehensive time-saving survey and research service (including questionnaire design, detailed analysis of data and a full written report). Provides schools and academies with impartial evidence for use in school self-evaluation and in the monitoring of school improvement initiatives.
https://edsrs.org.uk

Keele University School Surveys
Provides research support to schools.
www.keele.ac.uk/cfss

Kirkland Rowell Surveys
Provides a survey service to monitor parental, pupil, staff (including an optional governor analysis) perceptions.
www.gl-performance.co.uk/products/kirkland-rowell-surveys

Parent View Ofsted
Gives parents the opportunity to tell Ofsted what they think about their child's school.
https://parentview.ofsted.gov.uk

School Survey Experts
Provides surveys for staff, parents and pupils which will provide feedback for schools' self-evaluation and preparation for Ofsted inspection.
www.schoolsurveyexperts.co.uk

School Surveys
Designs and runs Internet surveys for your school or group. They provide all the facilities necessary for managing a survey while it is running and then for analysing or downloading the results.
www.schoolsurveys.co.uk

Survey Monkey
Creates and sends any type of survey with an easy-to-use survey builder.
www.surveymonkey.com

Research

DIY Evaluation Guide
A resource for teachers and schools which introduces the key principles of educational evaluation and provides practical advice on designing and carrying out small-scale evaluations in schools. It provides straightforward advice on how to complete the eight steps necessary for a DIY evaluation.
www.educationendowmentfoundation.org.uk

National Academy for Parenting Research
Has an internationally recognised research programme to help bring real change to the way practitioners work.
www.kcl.ac.uk/ioppn/depts/cap/research/NAPR/index.aspx

National Occupational Standards for Work with Parents
Nationally agreed statements of competence which describe what an effective and competent worker does and needs to know to deliver quality in their job.
www.parentinguk.org/your-work/what-is-work-with-parents/national-occupational-standards-for-work-with-parents/

Sutton Trust
As well as being a think-tank, the Sutton Trust is a 'do-tank'. The Trust identifies and pilots programmes to help non-privileged children, undertakes independent and robust evaluations, and scales up successful programmes, often on a national scale.
www.suttontrust.com

School systems

Behaviour Watch
A web-based system which allows schools to centralise their own recording systems and log behavioural incidents online.
www.behaviourwatch.co.uk

Class Dojo
Provides an online system for teachers to encourage students and share their best moments with parents.
www.classdojo.com

Frog Education
Allows parents to view, like and comment on their child's work direct from their dashboard.
www.frogeducation.com/products

Go 4 Schools
Online system designed to capture, analyse and share classroom data in real time and communicate to parents.
www.go4schools.com

IRIS Schools Data Services Ltd
An online behaviour and rewards solution for secondary schools.
www.adaptsoft.co.uk/solutions/education/secondary/index-iris.html

RIX Wiki
RIX Wiki provides a media tool for people with learning disabilities, their families, carers, and support professionals.
www.rixwiki.org/

Show My Homework
Allows teachers to quickly set simple homework tasks.
www.showmyhomework.co.uk

SIMS InTouch
Uses a combination of email, text messages and instant alerts to send information to parents, students and staff.
www.capita-sims.co.uk/products/sims-intouch-school-communication-tool

Spice Time Credits
Rewards for parents.
www.justaddspice.org

Social media and apps

Buffer
Social media dashboard.
https://buffer.com

Hootsuite
Social media dashboard.
https://hootsuite.com

Photocard
Create unique custom-designed postcards.
https://itunes.apple.com/us/app/photocard-by-bill-atkinson/id333208430?mt=8

Pinterest
Online visual discovery boards for projects and interests.
https://uk.pinterest.com

SocialOomph
Social media dashboard.
www.socialoomph.com

Tellagami
A mobile app to create animated messages.
www.tellagami.com

Supporting learning

BBC Parenting
Includes hints and tips for parents from experts in their fields on everything from dealing with teenagers and sibling rivalry to helping with homework.
www.bbc.co.uk/parenting

Digital Accessible Information System
The DAISY Consortium is a global partnership of organisations committed to creating the best way to read and publish, for everyone.
www.daisy.org

Edublogs
A free, safe blogging platform for teachers, students and school communities which keeps parents up to date with their child's education.
http://edublogs.org

Kidblog
Provides teachers with the tools to help students publish writing safely online so that parents can access.
https://kidblog.org

Literacy Trust
The Literacy Trust has produced the Words for Life website full of activities and resources for parents to help their children with literacy skills.
www.wordsforlife.org.uk

National Challenge Numeracy
Helps adults learn the maths needed in everyday life.
www.nnchallenge.org.uk

National Numeracy
Provides support and services for teachers and parents.
www.nationalnumeracy.org.uk

Storynory
Has hundreds of free audio stories.
www.storynory.com

Top Marks
Articles written by practising teachers designed to help with the education of your child.
www.topmarks.co.uk/parents.aspx

Toolkits/schemes

Engage Toolkit
Website supporting black and minority ethnic (BME) family carers.
www.engagetoolkit.org.uk

FaCE (Family and Community Engagement) Toolkit
A free family and community engagement toolkit for schools produced by the Welsh Assembly Government.
http://learning.gov.wales/resources/browse-all/family-and-community-engagement-toolkit

Family Engagement Officer's Toolkit
A toolkit for Family Engagement Officers produced by NSM Training & Consultancy.
www.nsmtc.co.uk/products

Training

NSM Training & Consultancy Ltd
Provides training and consultancy on all aspects of parent engagement within your school.
www.nsmtc.co.uk

References

Addi-Raccah, A. and Ainhoren, R. (2009) 'School governance and teachers' attitudes to parents' involvement in schools', *Teaching and Teacher Education*, 25: 805-13.

Aronson, J. Z. (1996) 'How schools can recruit hard-to-reach parents', *Educational Leadership*, 53(7): 58-60.

Baile, W. F., Buckman, R., Lenzi, R., Glober, G., Beale, E. A. and Kudelka, A. P. (2000) 'SPIKES – a six-step protocol for delivering bad news: application to the patient with cancer', *The Oncologist*, 5(4): 302-11.

Bastiani, J. (2003) *Materials for Schools: Involving Parents, Raising Achievement.* London: Department for Education and Skills. Available online at http://webarchive.nationalarchives.gov.uk/20130401151715/ http://www.education.gov.uk/publications/eOrderingDownload/PICE-IPRA.pdf (accessed 13 May 2016).

Battle-Bailey, L., Silvern, S. B., Brabham, E. and Ross, M. (2004) 'The effects of interactive reading homework and parent involvement on children's inference responses', *Early Childhood Education Journal*, 32(3): 173-8.

Bogenschneider, K. and Johnson, C. (2004) 'Family involvement in education: how important is it? What can legislators do?', in K. Bogenschneider and E. Gross (eds), *A Policymaker's Guide to School Finance: Approaches to Use and Questions to Ask*, Wisconsin Family Impact Seminar Briefing Report No. 20. Madison, WI: University of Wisconsin Center for Excellence in Family Studies.

Bojuwoye, O. (2009) 'Home-school partnership: a study of opinions of selected parents and teachers in Kwazulu Natal Province, South Africa', *Research Papers in Education: Policy and Practice*, 24(4): 461-75.

Buckman, R. (1992) *Breaking Bad News: A Guide for Health Care Professionals.* Baltimore, MD: Johns Hopkins University Press.

Care Quality Commission (2013) *Supporting Information and Guidance: Supporting Effective Clinical Supervision.* Available online at http://www.cqc.org.uk/sites/default/files/documents/20130625_800734_ v1_00_supporting_information-effective_clinical_supervision_for_publication.pdf (accessed 10 May 2016).

Clark, C. (2009) *Why Fathers Matter to Their Children's Literacy.* London: National Literacy Trust.

Coe, R., Kime, S., Nevill, C. and Coleman, R. (2013) *The DIY Evaluation Guide.* Education Endowment Foundation. Available online at https://v1.educationendowmentfoundation.org.uk/uploads/pdf/EEF_ DIY_Evaluation_Guide_(2013).pdf (accessed 10 May 2016).

Cotton, K. and Wikelund, K. R. (1989) *Parent Involvement in Education*, Education North West School Improvement Series (SIRS) Close-Up No. 6. Available online at http://educationnorthwest.org/sites/ default/files/ParentInvolvementinEducation.pdf (accessed 10 May 2016).

Crozier, G. and Davies, J. (2005) *'The Trouble is They Don't Mix': Self-Segregation or Enforced Exclusion? Asian Students Respond to Their Critics.* Paper presented to British Educational Research Association Conference, University of Glamorgan, September.

Dalziel, D. and Henthorne, K. (2005) *Parents'/Carers' Attitudes towards School Attendance*, Research Report No. 618. London: Department for Education and Skills.

Davis, H. and Meltzer, L. (2007) *Working in Partnership Through Early Support: Distance Learning Text: Working with Parents in Partnership.* Department for Education and Skills. Available online at http://dera.ioe.ac.uk/1928/1/working%20with%20parents%20in%20partnership.pdf (accessed 10 May 2016).

Davis, H. and Rushton, R. (1991) 'Counselling and supporting parents of children with developmental delay: a research evaluation', *Journal of Mental Deficiency Research*, 35: 89–112.

Davis, H. and Spurr, P. (1998) 'Parent counselling: an evaluation of a community child mental health service', *Journal of Child Psychology and Psychiatry*, 39: 365–76.

Day, C. and Davis, H. (2009) *The Family Partnership Reflective Practice Handbook*. London: CPCS.

Department for Education (2009) *How Schools Help Parents to Improve Children's Learning*. London: DfE.

Department for Education (2016) *Behaviour and Discipline in Schools: Advice for Headteachers and School Staff*. DfE.

Department for Education and Department of Health (2015) *Special Educational Needs and Disability Code of Practice: 0 to 25 Years. Statutory Guidance for Organisations which Work with and Support Children and Young People Who Have Special Educational Needs or Disabilities*. Available online at www.gov.uk/government/uploads/system/uploads/attachment_data/file/398815/SEND_Code_of_Practice_January_2015.pdf (accessed 10 May 2016).

Desforges, C. and Abouchaar, A. (2003) *The Impact of Parental Involvement, Parental Support and Family Education on Pupil Achievements and Adjustment: A Literature Review*. Available online at http://bgfl.org/bgfl/custom/files_uploaded/uploaded_resources/18617/Desforges.pdf (accessed 10 May 2016).

Douglas, H. (2004) *Solihull Approach Resource Pack, The School Years, For Care Professionals Who Work with School-Aged Children, Young People and Their Parents*. Solihull: National Health Service Care Trust.

Dunlop, A.-W. and Fabian, H. (eds) (2007) *Informing Transitions in the Early Years: Research, Policy and Practice*. Maidenhead: Open University Press.

Dweck, C. (2012) *Mindset: How You Can Fulfil Your Potential*. London: Robinson.

Edwards, K., Ellis, D., Ko, L., Saifer, S. and Stuczynski, A. (in press) *Classroom to Community and Back: Using Culturally Responsive Standards-Based (CRSB) Teaching to Strengthen Family and Community Partnerships and Increase Student Achievement*. Portland, OR: Northwest Regional Educational Laboratory.

Edwards, P.A. (2006) *Engaging Hard to Reach Parents*. PowerPoint presentation, Michigan State University.

Ellis, G. and Morgan, N. S. (2009) *The Family Values Scheme*. Cardiff: Behaviour Stop Ltd.

Ellis, G., Morgan, N. S. and Reid, K. (2013) *Better Behaviour Through Home-School Relations*. London: Routledge.

Epstein, J. L., Coates, L., Salinas, K. C., Sanders, M. G. and Simon, B. S. (1997) *School, Family and Community Partnerships: Your Handbook for Action*. Thousand Oaks, CA: Corwin.

Fan, X. and Chen, M. (2001) 'Parental involvement and student's academic achievement: a meta-analysis', *Educational Psychology Review*, 13(1): 1–22.

Geddes, H. (2008) 'Reflections on the role and significance of fathers in relation to emotional development and learning', *British Journal of Guidance and Counselling*, 36: 399–409.

Gershuny, J. (2000) *Changing Times: Work and Leisure in Post-Industrial Societies*. Oxford: Oxford University Press.

Gibbs, G. (1988) 'Reflective cycle', in *Learning by Doing: A Guide to Teaching and Learning Methods*. Oxford: Further Education Unit, Oxford Polytechnic.

Goodall, J. and Vorhaus, J. (2011) *Review of Best Practice in Parental Engagement: Practitioners Summary*. London: Department for Education. Available online at http://dera.ioe.ac.uk/11926/1/DFE-RR156.pdf (accessed 10 May 2016).

Hall, E. T. (1976) 'Edward T. Hall's Cultural Iceberg Model', from E. T. Hall, *Beyond Culture*. Available online at https://equity.spps.org/uploads/iceberg_model_3.pdf (accessed 10 May 2016).

Harris, A. and Goodall, J. (2006) *Engaging Parents in Raising Achievement: Do Parents Know They Matter?* University of Warwick research project, commissioned by the Specialist Schools and Academies Trust, funded by the DCSF. Available online at http://webarchive.nationalarchives.gov.uk/20130401151715/http://www.education.gov.uk/publications/eOrderingDownload/DCSF-RBW004.pdf (accessed 10 May 2016).

Harris, A. and Goodall, J. (2007) *Do Parents Know They Matter? A Research Project Commissioned by the Specialist Schools and Academies Trust*, Research Report DCSF-RW004. Available online at http://dera.ioe.ac.uk/6639/1/DCSF-RW004.pdf (accessed 10 May 2016).

Harris, A. and Goodall, J. (2009) *Helping Families Support Children's Success at School*. London: Save the Children Fund. Available online at www.savethechildren.org.uk/sites/default/files/docs/Helping_Families_Review_of_Research_Evidence_%285%29_1.pdf (accessed 10 May 2016).

Harris, A., Goodall, J. S. and Andrew-Powers, K. (2009) *Do Parents Know They Matter? Raising Achievement Through Parental Engagement*. New York: Continuum International.

Hattie, J. (2009) *Visible Learning: A Synthesis of Over 800 Meta-Analyses Relating to Achievement*. Abingdon: Routledge.

Howard, P. and CfBT Education Trust (2009) *Restorative Practice in Schools*. Available online at http://learning.gov.wales/docs/learningwales/publications/121129restorativepracticeen.pdf (accessed 10 May 2016).

Hutchins, D. J., Greenfield, M. D., Epstein, J. L., Sanders, M. G. and Galindo, C. L. (2012) *Multicultural Partnerships Involve All Families*. Larchmont, NY: Eye On Education.

Keatinge, D., Fowler, C. and Briggs, C. (2008) 'Evaluating the Family Partnership Model (FPM) program and implementation in practice in New South Wales, Australia', *Australian Journal of Advanced Nursing*, 25(2): 28–35.

Lamb, B. (2009) *Lamb Inquiry: Special Educational Needs and Parental Confidence*. Available online at http://webarchive.nationalarchives.gov.uk/20130401151715/https://www.education.gov.uk/publications/eOrderingDownload/01143-2009DOM-EN.pdf (accessed 10 May 2016).

Maschinot, B. (2008) *The Changing Face of the United States: The Influence of Culture on Early Child Development*. Washington, DC: Zero to Three, National Center for Infants, Toddlers, and Families. Available online at http://main.zerotothree.org/site/DocServer/Culture_book.pdf?docID=6921 (accessed 10 May 2016).

Mehrabian, A. (1972) *Nonverbal Communication*. Chicago: Aldine-Atherton.

Melhuish, E., Sylva, C., Sammons, P., Siraj-Blatchford, I. and Taggart, B. (2001) *Social, Behavioural and Cognitive Development at 3–4 Years in Relation to Family Background*. London: DfEE/Institute of Education, University of London.

Morgan, N. S. (2009) *Quick, Easy and Effective Behaviour Management Ideas for the Classroom*. London: Jessica Kingsley.

Morgan, N. S. (2014) *The Family Engagement Officer's Toolkit*. Cardiff: NSM Training & Consultancy Ltd.

Morgan, N. S. and Ellis, G. (2009) *The 5-Step Behaviour Programme: A Whole-School Approach to Behaviour Management*. Cardiff: Behaviour Stop Ltd.

Morgan, N. S. and Ellis, G. (2011) *A Kit Bag for Promoting Positive Behaviour in the Classroom*. London: Jessica Kingsley.

Morgan, N. S. and Ellis, G. (2012) *Good Choice Teddy Approach*. Monmouth: Good Choice Teddy Ltd.

O'Mara, A., Jamal, F., Llewellyn, A., Lehmann, A. and Cooper, C. (2010) *Improving Children's and Young People's Outcomes Through Support for Mothers, Fathers, and Carers*. Centre for Excellence and Outcomes in Children and Young People's Services (C4EO). Available online at http://archive.c4eo.org.uk/themes/families/effectivesupport/files/effective_support_research_review.pdf (accessed 13 May 2016).

OECD (2012) *Let's Read Them a Story! The Parent Factor in Education*. Pisa: OECD Publishing. Available online at http://dx.doi.org/10.1787/9789264176232-en (accessed 13 May 2016).

Page, J., Whitting, G. and McLean, C. (2008) *Engaging Effectively with Black and Minority Ethnic Parents in Children's and Parental Services*, Research Report DCSF-RR013. London: Department for Children, Schools and Families. Available online at http://webarchive.nationalarchives.gov.uk/20130401151715/http://www.education.gov.uk/publications/eorderingdownload/dcsf-rr013.pdf (accessed 10 May 2016).

Potter, C., Walker, G. and Keen, B. (2012) 'Engaging fathers from disadvantaged areas in children's early educational transitions: a UK perspective', *Journal of Early Childhood Research*, 10(2): 209–25.

Reid, K. and Morgan, N. S. (2012) *Tackling Behaviour in Your Primary School*. London: Routledge.

Riley, K. (2009) 'Reconfiguring urban leadership: taking a perspective on community', *School Leadership and Management*, 29(1): 51–63.

Rogers, S. (2009) *Education Child Protection Manager*. Cambridgeshire Local Safeguarding Children Board.

Rutter, M., Maughan, B., Mortimore, P. and Ouston, J. (1979) *Fifteen Thousand Hours: Secondary Schools and Their Effects on Children*. London: Open Books.

Sammons, P., Sylva, K., Melhuish, E., Siraj-Blatchford, I. *et al.* (2007) *The Influence of School and Teaching Quality on Children's Progress in Primary School*. London: Department for Children, Schools and Families. Available online at http://webarchive.nationalarchives.gov.uk/20130401151715/http://www.education.gov.uk/publications/eOrderingDownload/DCSF-RR028.pdf (accessed 10 May 2016).

Samway, K. D. and McKeon, D. (2007) *Myths and Realities: Best Practices for English Language Learners*, 2nd edn. Portsmouth, NH: Heinemann.

Scottish Executive (2006) *Guidance on the Scottish Schools (Parental Involvement) Act 2006*. Edinburgh: Scottish Executive.

Scottish Government (2006) *Guidance for Education Authorities, Parent Councils and Others on the Scottish Schools (Parental Involvement) Act 2006*. Available online at http://www.gov.scot/Publications/2006/09/08094112/0 (accessed 13 May 2016).

Skills for Care (2007) *Providing Effective Supervision: A Workforce Development Tool, Including a Unit of Competence and Supporting Guidance*. Available online at www.skillsforcare.org.uk/Document-library/Finding-and-keeping-workers/Supervision/Providing-Effective-Supervision.pdf (accessed 10 May 2016).

Trumbull, E. and Pacheco, M. (2005) *The Teacher's Guide to Diversity: Building a Knowledge Base*. Providence, RI: Education Alliance at Brown University.

Trumbull, E., Rothstein-Fisch, C. and Hernandez, E. (n.d.) 'Parent involvement in schooling – according to whose values?', *School Community Journal*. Available online at http://www.adi.org/journal/fw03/Trumbull,%20et%20al.pdf (accessed 10 May 2016).

Weiss, H. B., Bouffard, S. M., Bridglall, B. L. and Gordon, E.W. (2009) *Reframing Family Involvement in Education: Supporting Families to Support Educational Equity*. New York: Columbia University Press. Available online at www.equitycampaign.org/i/a/document/12018_equitymattersvol5_web.pdf (accessed 10 May 2016).

Welsh Assembly Government (2014) *Family and Community Engagement Toolkit for Schools, Theme 3: Welcoming Families to Engage with the School, Resources 1–9*. Available online at http://learning.gov.wales/docs/learningwales/publications/150729-theme3-en.pdf (accessed 10 May 2016).

Williams, F. and Churchill, H. (2006) *National Evaluation Report November 2006, Empowering Parents in Sure Start Local Programmes*. Available online at http://www.ness.bbk.ac.uk/implementation/documents/1385.pdf (accessed 10 May 2016).

Wilson, H. and Huntington, A. (2009) *An Exploration of the Family Partnership Model in New Zealand*, Blue Skies Report No. 27/09. Wellington: Families Commission.

Index